ACTS

Power for Witnessing

A BIBLE CORRESPONDENCE COURSE

Text Material by
ALFRED MARTIN, Th.D.
Vice-President and Dean of Education
Moody Bible Institute

Arranged as a Correspondence Course
by
MOODY CORRESPONDENCE SCHOOL

MOODY BIBLE INSTITUTE
CORRESPONDENCE SCHOOL
820 North LaSalle Street
Chicago, Illinois 60610

Instructions to Students

The book of Acts is one of the key books in the Bible. During the period it covers, Judaism was superseded by Christianity. Beginning in an upper room in Jerusalem, the church spread until, by the time Luke laid down his pen, there was a church in every major city of the Roman Empire. The book of Acts traces the growth and progress of the church until the time Paul, the great apostle to the Gentiles, reached Rome. It is a book of people, places and principles. It forms a vital bridge between the Gospels and the epistles. As you study it, you will feel the pulse of the vigorous, dynamic Christianity of the first century and, we trust, will feel your own pulse quicken in response.

HOW THE COURSE IS ORGANIZED

LESSON

HOW LONG SHOULD IT TAKE?

Study at your own speed. Normally, about two hours are required to complete a lesson. You should aim to complete one lesson each week and mail your exams regularly.

HOW TO STUDY

Try to find a quiet spot free from distractions and noise, in order to concentrate on your work. Have a pencil with you and underline or mark important words or passages. Look in a dictionary for any words you do not understand.

Since the Bible is God's Book, you need the help of the Holy Spirit if you are to understand it. Psalm 119:18, if prayed from the heart, would be an appropriate prayer to use: "Open thou mine eyes, that I may behold wondrous things out of thy law."

Follow the order of study outlined at the beginning of each lesson. There are four steps you should take:

1. Read Your Bible

Each lesson in the textbook covers a certain number of chapters in the book of Acts. Read the assigned chapters from the Bible at least twice. First, read them quickly, skimming to get an over-all impression of what they contain. Second, read the chapters slowly to pick up the details.

2. Self-Check Tests

You will get the best results from this course by reading and studying the book of Acts itself. Each lesson is therefore preceded by a preparatory self-check test based on the assigned Scripture portion. *Always take the self-check test before reading the lesson in the textbook.* This is important, because it will help you get your own first impressions of the Scripture portion to be studied.

Here is how to take the preparatory self-check test. On your second reading of the assigned Scripture portion, use the self-check test questions as an aid to personal study. When you have finished studying the Scripture passages and think you can answer the self-check test questions, do so without reference to the Bible. When you have finished the self-check test, correct your answers using the answer key at the end of the course.

You can do the preparatory self-check tests the night before you study your textbook lesson if you wish. You may prefer to incorporate your reading assignments in Acts and self-check tests into your daily quiet time. However, be sure to take these tests *before* reading the lesson in the textbook.

3. SQ3R

When you have done the preparatory self-check test preceding a given lesson, you are ready to study what the textbook has to say about the assigned chapters from Acts. To help you in your study, remember this simple formula *SQ3R*. It spells out five effective steps to take to fix the content of each lesson firmly in your mind. These symbols *SQ3R* stand for SURVEY, QUESTIONS, READ, RECITE, REVIEW. You will find the SQ3R *formula* boxed in at the beginning of every lesson and the SQ3R *questions* boxed in at the end of every lesson. Here's how to make SQ3R work for you.

Survey   Glance over the topical headings in the lesson. These are printed in bold face type. It should take you less than a minute. You will get the core ideas around which the lesson is built.

Questions At the end of each lesson, boxed in from the main text you will find some questions. These will arouse your curiosity. They will help

5

make the main points you are to learn stand out in your mind.

Read Seek to answer the questions as you read. This way you will become an active learner, instead of a passive reader.

Recite After each section, put down your book and recite back what you have learned. Use your own words. Can you answer the questions asked? Jot down cue phrases in outline form on a sheet of paper.

Review Cover up all your notes. Recall from memory the main points of the lesson. Answer all the questions asked in the box at the end of the lesson.

4. Exams

After every second lesson, you will find a complete exam covering the two preceding lessons and marked accordingly. Turn to this exam after you have applied SQ3R to your study of the lesson and see how well you know the answers. You may take the exam in two stages if you wish, that is, one lesson at a time. However, do not send in an exam until both sections (covering two lessons) are completed.

Glance through the lesson until you are sure you can answer all the questions on the exam, or section of the exam. When you are sure you can do this, you are ready for the exam.

a. **Write the exam.** Complete it according to instructions and without referring to your textbook or notes. Use pen and dark ink. Use your Bible if instructions tell you to do so.

b. **Detach the exam.** When you have completed both sections of the exam (that is, when you have answered all the questions you can relating to two lessons), detach the exam from your textbook. If you are

6

careful, you will find that the pages may be taken out without spoiling your textbook.

c. Mail your exam to the Correspondence School. Do this as soon as you complete both sections of each exam.

d. Keep your exams for future use. To keep your exams for future reference, put them in a three-ring notebook. You will find the ring marks indicated on your exam sheets.

RECORD YOUR GRADES

At the front of the book you will find a Grade Record Card. Each time you receive a corrected exam from the Correspondence School make a careful note of the grade in the appropriate place on the card. When sending in your *last* exam, return this Grade Record Card to the Correspondence School so that you may be issued a certificate. Make sure that all grades are recorded on this card with the exception of the final exam(s) you are enclosing. This is important.

CLASS ENROLLMENTS

If you are enrolled in a class, submit your exam papers to the leader or secretary of the class, who will send them for the group to the Correspondence School.

Class leaders are to print or type the names of all students enrolled in the course on the Class Record Sheet. Before returning corrected exams to the students, the class leader must record the grades on the Class Record Sheet. Each student should also keep a record of his own grades on the Grade Record Card found in the front of each textbook. When the last exam is taken, the completed Class Record Sheet must be returned to the Correspondence School. The grades of *all* completed exams must be recorded, with the exception of the final ones being returned with the Class Record Sheet. For example, if you are sending in Exam 6 for correction, the Class Record Sheet must show the grades of Exams 1-5 for all students who have completed them. If a student finishes the course after the Class Record Sheet has been sent in, he should send his completed Grade Record Card to the Correspondence School. This card must bear an accurate record of the student's *grades, class number* and *signature.*

GENERAL INSTRUCTIONS

1. Each exam is made up of twenty parts, each of which is valued at five points. Upon completing the course with a passing grade of 70 percent or more, you will be awarded a certificate.

2. The King James Version is used in this course, except for a possible quotation from the American Standard Version, published in 1901. These quotations are indicated by the abbreviation, A.S.V.

3. The Correspondence School staff meets weekly for prayer on behalf of the students. These dedicated workers consider it a privilege to share with you your prayer requests. Please write requests on a separate sheet of paper and send them with your exams.

4. You will be allowed one year to complete the course from the time of enrollment. Your name will then be removed from the roll and you will be able to earn a certificate for the course only by complete re-enrollment.

What the Lord Jesus Continued to Do

The Citadel of David, Jerusalem.

YOUR STUDY GUIDE

1. Read the assigned Scripture portion.

2. Take the self-check test based on the Scripture portion.

3. Study the lesson using SQ3R:
   a. Survey the lesson.
   b. Read the SQ3R questions at the end of the lesson.
   c. Read the lesson.
   d. Recite the lesson making marginal notations.
   e. Review the lesson by answering the SQ3R questions boxed in at the end of the lesson.

4. Take the exam.

SCRIPTURE PORTION FOR STUDY

Read Acts 1 and 2 twice and then take the following self-check test. Look up the answers to questions in the answer key on page 147.

SELF-CHECK TEST 1

In the right-hand margin check (√) the following statements "True" or "False" based on your reading of the assigned Scripture portion.

	T	F
1. The writer of Acts could find very little substantial evidence for Christ's resurrection.		√
2. Before His ascension, the Lord gave specific instructions for the evangelization of the world.	√	
3. The ascension of Christ took place in the city of Jerusalem.		√
4. Matthias was appointed successor to Judas by Simon Peter.		√
5. The manifestation of the Holy Spirit on the Day of Pentecost was in tongues as of fire and a sound as of a rushing wind.	√	
6. The "tongues" exhibited on the Day of Pentecost were unintelligible to the foreigners in Jerusalem.		√
7. Peter claimed that the phenomena observed on the Day of Pentecost were predicted in a prophecy of Joel.	√	
8. About three thousand people were saved on the Day of Pentecost.	√	
9. Those saved on the Day of Pentecost were baptized and continued in the teachings of the apostles.	√	
10. It was a long time after Pentecost before any more souls were saved and added to the church.		√

Do not send the answers to these questions to the Correspondence School.

What the Lord Jesus Continued to Do

ACTS 1, 2

The book which is called the Acts of the Apostles was written by Luke as a continuation of his Gospel. In the introduction Luke tells us how in the "former treatise" he made known "all that Jesus began both to do and teach" (Acts 1:1). From this wording it is logical to assume that Acts tells of the continuing ministry of the risen Lord Jesus
10 Christ, working by His Holy Spirit through the apostles and other believers. We may look at the New Testament this way:

What "Jesus began both to do and teach"—the GOSPELS
What Jesus continued to *do*—the ACTS
What Jesus continued to *teach*—the EPISTLES and the REVELATION

We may expect then that this book will contain the record of some of those deeds which the Lord Jesus promised His disciples they would perform when He said:
20 "Verily, verily, I say unto you, He that believeth on me, the works that I do shall he do also; and greater works than these shall he do; because I go unto my Father" (John 14:12).

ACTS A BOOK OF WITNESSING

Acts is pre-eminently a book of witnessing, following the plan laid down by the Lord Jesus Christ in His last interview with the disciples before His ascension to heaven. He said:
"But ye shall receive power, after that the Holy Ghost is come upon you: and ye shall be witnesses unto me both in

Jerusalem, and in all Judea, and in Samaria, and unto the uttermost part of the earth" (Acts 1:8).

The first main division of the book tells of the witness in Jerusalem, Judea and Samaria (chapters 1—12) ; the second division tells of the witness to the ends of the earth (chapters 13—28).

ACTS A BOOK OF ACTIVE CHRISTIANS

The title of the book is not a part of the inspired text, but was given at a very early date. Actually we are told nothing in the book about the acts of most of the apostles. The majority are not mentioned after the listing of their names among those in the upper room before Pentecost (Acts 1:13).   *10*

The story in Acts revolves mainly around Peter and Paul. The first part describes the ministry of Peter and others, principally to Jews, from the center in Jerusalem (chapters 1—12). The second part portrays the ministry of Paul and others, principally to Gentiles, from the new center of missionary activity in Antioch (chapters 13—28).

Acts is a book of the stirring deeds of men and women   *20* filled with the Holy Spirit. While Peter and Paul dominate the record, attention is given to Stephen, the first martyr; Philip, the deacon and the evangelist of Samaria; Barnabas, the befriender of Paul; Silas, the missionary companion; Aquila and Priscilla, co-workers with Paul and instructors of Apollos; and others. Luke himself is there in the "we" sections (Acts 16:10-17; 20:6—21:18; 27:1—28:16).

ACTS A BOOK OF SPEECHES

Acts is a book of sermons and addresses, delivered on all sorts of occasions under widely varying circumstances, such   *30* as Peter's sermon on the Day of Pentecost (Acts 2:14-36); Stephen's address to the Sanhedrin (Acts 7:2-53), the longest in the book; Paul's message in the synagogue at Antioch in Pisidia (Acts 13:16-41); his farewell to the Ephesian elders at Miletus (Acts 20:18-35); his speech to the mob in Jerusalem (Acts 22:1-21); his defense before the governor Felix (Acts 24:10-21); and that before King Agrippa (Acts 26:1-29). In all, there are more than twenty-five public speeches recorded, at least in part, in the book. Almost half of these were delivered by the Apostle Paul.

ACTS A BOOK OF CITIES

Acts is a book of cities, because it is a book of missions, and the gospel was taken first to the centers of population in order that it might be dispersed from each center to the
10 surrounding areas. Jerusalem, Samaria and Antioch play their parts. Then the great cities of Asia Minor and of Greece come into view as the Apostle Paul travels on his extensive missionary journeys. Philippi, Athens, Corinth and Ephesus have an important place as Paul looks toward Rome, the capital of the empire and the symbol of the outreach of the gospel to the uttermost part of the earth. The book of Acts might almost be called (as at least one writer has titled his commentary on it) *From Jerusalem to Rome*.

ACTS A BOOK OF RESURRECTION

20 The preachers and witnesses in the book of Acts were vitally aware of the fact that they served a resurrected Lord. From the beginning of the book, where we see the risen Lord Himself instructing His disciples and showing "himself alive after his passion by many infallible proofs" (Acts 1:3), on to the very end, they preached "Jesus and the resurrection" (Acts 17:18). They had no truncated or incomplete gospel. Fully knowing and proclaiming the substitutionary death of the Lord Jesus Christ as the ground of salvation, they also held forth His bodily resurrection from
30 the dead as the climax and proof of His finished redemptive work. They served a living Saviour and Lord, whom they recommended to all they met. Because the messengers themselves partook of new life from their risen Lord, they had a message of life to those dead in trespasses and sins.

13

ACTS A BOOK OF THE HOLY SPIRIT

All through the book of Acts we observe the sovereign working of God the Holy Spirit empowering believers to be witnesses for the Lord Jesus as He had promised (Acts 1:8). This statement of the Lord just before His ascension is undoubtedly the key to the book. The promise was fulfilled at Pentecost and in all the events that followed. Power for witnessing throughout the world is the theme of the book, and that power was from the Holy Spirit, not mere human ability. Repeatedly we are told that He—the Holy Spirit— *10* filled the believers; that He directed the messengers where they should go and where they should not go; that He opened men's hearts. God the Father was working; God the Son, the Lord Jesus Christ, was working; God the Holy Spirit was working. Yes, it was God who was working, for the three Persons are all one and the selfsame God. The results were seen to be His, and the glory His. The believers were His servants, His instruments.

PREPARATION FOR WITNESSING (CHAPTER 1)

We are now to consider briefly the first two chapters of *20* Acts. In chapter 1 the believers are waiting for the Holy Spirit; in chapter 2 they are empowered by the Holy Spirit.

The Lord Jesus made it clear to His disciples that following His death and resurrection the Holy Spirit would begin new ministries in the world surpassing those He had accomplished before (compare John 7:37-39; 14:16, 17; 16:7-15; Acts 1:4-8). It was therefore right and necessary for those disciples immediately after the Lord's ascension to wait for the Holy Spirit, to wait for the fulfillment of the promise. There is no necessity now to wait, for the Holy Spirit has *30* come; He is here. At Pentecost He baptized the believers into one body, the body of Christ (compare Acts 1:5 with I Corinthians 12:13), and filled them for Christian living and witnessing.

Returning from the Mount of Olives from which they had watched the Lord Jesus ascend to heaven, the disciples

14

gathered for prayer and fellowship in an upper room. Many students of Scripture believe that this may have been the same upper room in which the Lord had eaten the Last Supper with His disciples.

The "one accord" (Acts 1:14) of the eleven and of the 120 believers generally led to earnest prayer and waiting upon God. During this time of waiting a successor to Judas Iscariot, the betrayer of the Lord Jesus, was chosen from the group. Although some have questioned the procedure, 10 the believers seem to have followed the proper order as indicated in the Old Testament for discerning the leading of God (see, for example, Proverbs 16:33). After Pentecost we read no more of the casting of lots in this fashion. Some have denied that Matthias was God's choice, arguing that he is never heard of again. But neither are most of the Twelve heard of again in the Scripture. There is no indication in the record that God disapproved of what was done, but quite the contrary.

It is sometimes said that God set aside Matthias and 20 chose Paul to be among the apostles. This is definitely a misunderstanding. Paul always asserted that he had a special apostleship, pertaining primarily to the Gentiles. He never considered himself one of the Twelve, although he was truly an apostle, commissioned directly by the risen Lord (see Galatians 1:1-12).

THE DAY OF PENTECOST (CHAPTER 2)

Pentecost ("fiftieth") was the Old Testament Feast of Weeks, coming on the fiftieth day after the Feast of First Fruits at the spring harvest. On that occasion the loaves 30 made from the grain of the harvest were offered before the Lord. In the New Testament fulfillment of the Old Testament typology, the Lord Jesus Christ in His resurrection was the first fruits (I Corinthians 15:20). Pentecost is the birthday of the church, the new body which the Lord Jesus was forming for Himself (Matthew 16:18; Acts 15:14; I Corinthians 12:13; Ephesians 1:22, 23; 2:19—3:7).

The Holy Spirit supernaturally empowered the believers

15

to speak in other languages which they had not learned, in order that the people from the different areas named in the account might hear the gospel in their own tongues. This is the true gift of tongues, given by the Holy Spirit in the early days of the church for the furtherance of the gospel—far different from the ecstatic utterances which are claimed by some to be the gift of tongues today.

Peter's sermon emphasized that it was the Lord Jesus Christ, delivered by God's purpose, slain by wicked hands, raised from the dead by God and exalted, who had sent the *10* Holy Spirit as manifested at that time. The prophecy of Joel began to have its fulfillment in the events of Pentecost (compare Joel 2:28-32 with Acts 2:16-21).

Three thousand persons came to the Lord Jesus Christ that day (Acts 2:41). The promise of the Lord was being fulfilled. The Holy Spirit had come upon the believers; they had been empowered; and they had become witnesses for the Lord Jesus in Jerusalem. The closing verses of chapter 2 tell of the stirring events of those days, the awe and wonder, the joy and gladness, the fellowship and praise to God, *20* and God's daily addition to the church.

SQ3R   LESSON 1

Before studying this lesson, see the instructions on page 5 for making use of the SQ3R formula. These questions should be used in your study.

1. Why can Acts be called a book of witnessing?

   _____

2. Who are the two chief characters in the book?

   _____

3. What prominence is given to speeches in Acts?

   _____

4. What is the role of the Holy Spirit in Acts?

   _____

5. Why is Acts 1:8 regarded as the key verse of the book?

   _____

6. What did the disciples do between the ascension and the Day of Pentecost?

   _____

7. What significant events took place on the Day of Pentecost?

   _____

Early Preaching in Jerusalem

Aerial picture of the Old City, Jerusalem.
Jordan Tourist Attache, N.Y.

YOUR STUDY GUIDE

1. Read the assigned Scripture portion.

2. Take the self-check test based on the Scripture portion.

3. Study the lesson using SQ3R:
   a. Survey the lesson.
   b. Read the SQ3R questions at the end of the lesson.
   c. Read the lesson.
   d. Recite the lesson making marginal notations.
   e. Review the lesson by answering the SQ3R questions boxed in at the end of the lesson.

4. Take the exam.

SCRIPTURE PORTION FOR STUDY

Read Acts 3, 4 and 5 twice and then take the following self-check test. Look up the answers to questions in the answer key on page 147.

SELF-CHECK TEST 2

*In the right-hand margin check (√) the following state-
ments "True" or "False" based on your reading of the
assigned Scripture portion.*

	T	F
1. The man healed by Peter had been lame from birth.	√	
2. The lame man once he was healed slipped away into the crowds.		√
3. Peter told the assembled multitudes that he had healed the lame man by his own power.		√
4. Peter and John were very much afraid of the Sanhedrin (i.e., the ruling Jewish court) before which they were arraigned.		√
5. The Sanhedrin decided the best way to combat Peter's influence in Jerusalem was to deny that he had performed the miracle.		√
6. Barnabas was one of those in the early church who sold his property and placed the proceeds into the communal fund.	√	
7. Ananias and Sapphira fully followed the example set by others in the church and gave all their possessions to the common fund.		√
8. The experience of Ananias and Sapphira put fear into the hearts of the believers.	√	
9. The apostles, arrested by the Sanhedrin, were miraculously released from prison by an angel.	√	
10. Gamaliel urged the Sanhedrin to use caution and moderation in dealing with the Christians.	√	

*Do not send the answers to these questions to the Corre-
spondence School.*

Early Preaching in Jerusalem

ACTS 3—5

Following the Day of Pentecost the Holy Spirit continued to use the apostles and other believers in the city of Jerusalem. The promise of the Lord Jesus (Acts 1:8) continued to be fulfilled. We read of this testimony:

"And with great power gave the apostles witness of the resurrection of the Lord Jesus: and great grace was upon
10 them all" (Acts 4:33).

The book of Acts by its very nature is crammed with action. Stirring events crowd upon one another without letup. These chapters (3—5) which continue the story of the early preaching in Jerusalem are no exception. Note, for example, the far-reaching results of the miracle of the healing of the lame man.

A NOTABLE MIRACLE (Acts 4:16)

The miracles recorded in Acts were performed by God as evidence of the truth of the witness given by the believers.
20 God confirmed "the word with signs following" (Mark 16:20). As we read these chapters of Acts, we need to allow ourselves to be caught up in the marvelous excitement of those days. As Paul was to say much later to Agrippa, "This thing was not done in a corner" (Acts 26:26). The events were public and they became public knowledge. In the face of the evident power of God, no one could long remain neutral. The amazement of the populace soon gave way to belief on the part of many, opposition on the part of others. The rulers particularly were troubled about the

21

fast-moving events, because they recognized that their prestige and influence were threatened. Consequently they lost no time, after the healing of the lame man at the Beautiful Gate and Peter's words to the crowd, in taking Peter and John into custody.

"Such as I have give I thee," said Peter to the lame man (Acts 3:6). We cannot give what we do not have. Often since then the church has lacked the power to do for men what they cannot do for themselves. Always this lack comes from failure to depend upon the risen Lord Jesus Christ, *10* who has sent the Holy Spirit to give power. "In the name of Jesus Christ of Nazareth rise up and walk" (Acts 3:6). Peter made it clear as he spoke to the people that he and John had no power of their own to do anything for the lame man. The power came from Christ. "And his name through faith in his name hath made this man strong" (Acts 3:16).

That the man had been lame and that now he could walk could not be denied by anyone. The only thing the leaders could do to stop the testimony was to try to suppress it by force, since they could not successfully refute it. *20*

PETER AND JOHN BEFORE THE COUNCIL

Just as Peter had preached Christ before the multitude, so he now proclaimed Him before the Sanhedrin, the council of religious leaders, showing from Psalm 118 that this One was the stone rejected by them, the builders, but exalted by God to be the "head of the corner" (Acts 4:11). Christ, declared Peter, is the only Saviour:

"Neither is there salvation in any other: for there is none other name under heaven given among men, whereby we must be saved" (Acts 4:12). *30*

The only solution the unbelieving religious leaders could propose was to command silence. But when God says, "Speak," and man says, "Be silent," God's servants have no choice but to speak (see Acts 4:19, 20; compare Acts 5:28, 29).

GREAT GRACE UPON THEM ALL

As the company of believers received Peter and John after their release, they praised God—quoting from Psalm 2—and prayed for boldness to speak of Christ. God answered their prayer (Acts 4:31). The promise of the Lord Jesus continued to be fulfilled; they were recipients of power through the Holy Spirit of God. With their enduement of power by the Holy Spirit they also experienced a oneness which led to their sharing with others all that they had.

10   Many have spoken of this situation in the early church as an ancient form of communism. It bears no relation to Marxist communism, which is atheistic and materialistic. There was no compulsion about what the believers did. Their actions were the outflow of Christian love. They did not demand that others share with them, as communists ordinarily do; they joyfully shared with others.

    There is no indication that any believer was obligated to turn in all his possessions to the apostles. "Great grace was upon them all" (Acts 4:33). Each man who brought his
20 property to the apostles for distribution did so from the inner prompting of the Spirit of God. The sin of Ananias and Sapphira was not in withholding that which was theirs; it was in pretending to give all, when they had given only a part. Genuine benevolence has its counterfeits. Ananias and his wife apparently wanted to keep part of their property for their own use and enjoyment, while at the same time gaining a reputation among the believers for total commitment of person and possessions.

CONTRAST IN THE CHURCH

30 At this point we first hear of Barnabas (Acts 4:36), who figures prominently later in the record. Here at the beginning he shows by his actions that character which is evident throughout, that "he was a good man, and full of the Holy Ghost and of faith" (Acts 11:24). His benevolence and beneficence are apparent in what he did (Acts 4:37). This man, filled with the Holy Spirit, is in contrast to the hypocrites, Ananias and Sapphira, who lied to the Holy Spirit

23

(Acts 5:3). The judgment from God which fell upon this couple brought fear to the church and no doubt deterred others from similar sinful acts. This is reminiscent of the sin of Achan in the early days of the nation of Israel (Joshua 7:1-26).

As the preaching of the gospel continued, God continued to give evidence of the truth of the message by miraculous signs (Acts 5:12-16). The result was a rapid increase in the number of believers and great excitement in the city of Jerusalem. *10*

PERSECUTION AGAIN

Such events could not go unnoticed by the religious leaders. The high priest and others of the Sadducean party brought about the arrest of the apostles. We can imagine the consternation of these frantic men when they were told that the ones whom they had put in prison were no longer there, although the doors were shut and the watchmen on guard; then to be told a little later that the elusive apostles were publicly preaching in the temple courts. These religious leaders could not admit that God was working in and *20* through the apostles. They did not know, and would not have admitted it if they had known, that an angel had opened the prison door.

As sometimes happens in the history of this mad world, the ordinary crowd had more sense than the leaders. The people at least recognized that God was somehow involved in all the unusual things that had been occurring in Jerusalem. Consequently the arresting officers had to bring the apostles this time "without violence" (Acts 5:26), "for they feared the people, lest they should have been stoned." *30*

The Lord Jesus Christ clearly commanded obedience to the state in its proper sphere when He said, "Render therefore unto Caesar the things which are Caesar's; and unto God the things that are God's" (Matthew 22:21). When Caesar comes into conflict with God, however, Caesar must yield:

24

"Then Peter and the other apostles answered and said, We ought to obey God rather than men" (Acts 5:29).

There is sometimes such a thing as a natural bravado, even at times a native heroism in the face of danger, but this was a supernatural boldness; this was the manifestation of the power given by the Holy Spirit. "Ye shall receive power," the Lord Jesus had said, and "ye shall be witnesses unto me." Peter and his associates realized this. "We are his witnesses of these things," they explained, "and so is also the Holy Ghost, whom God hath given to them that obey him" (Acts 5:32).

The response of the council was a murderous hatred that wanted to kill the apostles as they had killed the apostles' Lord. What the outcome would have been we cannot say had it not been for the counsel of moderation given by one of their own number, Gamaliel. Different reactions have been expressed by commentators about Gamaliel's advice. Whether he spoke from an awakening awareness of spiritual truth, or whether, as seems more likely, he was only voicing the worldly wisdom for which he was noted, his words had weight with the council. "Let them alone," was the substance of his message. "Let the results prove whether they are of God or not." It is doubtful that any of that number, including Gamaliel, really believed that this preaching was from God. They evidently expected the message to fade away, as the other examples whom Gamaliel cited had passed off the scene of history.

But they could not quite leave them alone. They beat the apostles, and "commanded that they should not speak in the name of Jesus, and let them go" (Acts 5:40). These rulers, who seemed to have so much power and who thought they were the guardians of the truth, might well have trembled as the apostles left their presence. How could they hope to prevail against those who rejoiced "that they were counted worthy to suffer shame for his name" and who daily "ceased not to teach and preach Jesus Christ" (Acts 5:41, 42)? The chief priests were indeed fighting against God!

25

When we think of the circumstances under which those early Christians lived and witnessed for the Lord Jesus, we may well ask ourselves about our testimony for Him.

SQ3R LESSON 2

Use these questions as you apply this formula to your study.

1. What took place at the Beautiful Gate of the temple?

   _____

2. How did the Jewish leaders react to this incident?

   _____

3. Was the communal living of the early church an early expression of communism?

   _____

4. How did Ananias and Sapphira sin against the Holy Spirit?

   _____

5. Do Christians have to obey rulers who command them not to witness for Christ?

   _____

6. How did the apostles react to persecution?

   _____

Stephen and Philip

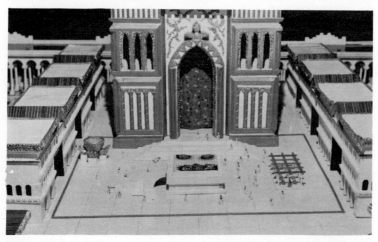

The inner court of the Jerusalem temple.

From a model by Fred W. Lawrence

YOUR STUDY GUIDE

1. Read the assigned Scripture portion.

2. Take the self-check test based on the Scripture portion.

3. Study the lesson using SQ3R:
   a. Survey the lesson.
   b. Read the SQ3R questions at the end of the lesson.
   c. Read the lesson.
   d. Recite the lesson making marginal notations.
   e. Review the lesson by answering the SQ3R questions boxed in at the end of the lesson.

4. Take the exam.

SCRIPTURE PORTION FOR STUDY

Read Acts 6, 7 and 8 twice and then take the following self-check test. Look up the answers to questions in the answer key on page 147.

SELF-CHECK TEST 3

In the right-hand margin check (√) the following state-ments "True" or "False" based on your reading of the assigned Scripture portion.

	T	F
1. The first seven deacons of the church were chosen by the apostles themselves.		√
2. Stephen was a man full of the Holy Ghost, wisdom, faith and power, and was a man of honest report.	√	
3. When they were unable to win their arguments, the Jews hired false witnesses to testify against Stephen.	√	
4. In his defense before the Sanhedrin, Stephen mentioned Abraham, Isaac, Jacob, Joseph, Pharaoh, Moses, Aaron, David, Solomon and Jesus.	√	
5. Before his martyrdom, Stephen saw the risen Lord standing at the right hand of God.	√	
6. Stephen called upon God to punish his murderers as he died.		√
7. Saul was so impressed with Stephen's defense of the gospel that he immediately sought to join the Jerusalem church.		√
8. Simon, the sorcerer of Samaria, was baptized as a result of the preaching of Philip.	√	
9. The Ethiopian eunuch was reading Isaiah 53:7, 8 when Philip asked him if he understood what he read.	√	
10. The Ethiopian eunuch was baptized after he returned to Ethiopia.		√

Do not send the answers to these questions to the Corre-spondence School.

Stephen and Philip

ACTS 6—8

The growing company of believers in Jerusalem, and consequent difficulties about the care of those in need, led to
the appointment of seven men to have oversight of the
"daily ministration" (Acts 6:1). While these men were
primarily to have responsibility for temporal needs, they
were also daily proclaimers of the gospel. Two in particular
were outstanding: Stephen, who became the first martyr
10   for Christ; and Philip, the evangelist of Samaria.

DEACONS CHOSEN

The occasion for the selection of the seven was the feeling
on the part of the Hellenists, or Greek-speaking Jews, that
their widows were being neglected. The apostles, recognizing their pre-eminent spiritual duties of prayer and the
ministry of the Word, called for the appointment of seven
men to oversee the care of temporal needs. Although the
word *deacons* is not used in this passage, its root form is
found in the verb translated "serve" tables (Acts 6:2).
20   From this beginning, apparently, the office of deacon developed.

Possibly all seven appointed were Hellenists, for they all
had Greek names. The apostles saw to it that there was no
discrimination in the distribution to those in need. There
is no further mention of complaint on the part of the church
concerning this matter.

We must be careful to note, however, that the spiritual
and the temporal cannot be separated. Even though the deacons were to provide for physical and material needs, they
30   were to be men "of honest report, full of the Holy Ghost
and wisdom" (Acts 6:3). We see that they did not confine

33

themselves to material concerns, but preached tirelessly and
fearlessly.

STEPHEN'S WITNESS AND ARREST

The first man chosen by the church is described particularly
as "full of faith and of the Holy Ghost" (Acts 6:5). Stephen
proclaimed Christ with such eloquence and power that his
adversaries, despairing of defeating him in debate, resorted
to fraud and force. The charges against him were calculated
to appeal to the deepest prejudices of the populace:

"We have heard him speak blasphemous words against 10
Moses, and against God. . . . For we have heard him say,
that this Jesus of Nazareth shall destroy this place, and
shall change the customs which Moses delivered us" (Acts
6:11, 14).

All the people's traditional reverence for Moses and for
the law was invoked by such charges as these.

Stephen stood before the council as the Lord Jesus Himself had stood some years before. No doubt some of the
same men sat there, and many of them were filled with the
same murderous hatred that had caused them to condemn 20
the "Prince of life" to death (compare Acts 3:15). There
was no sympathy in this company for this man with "the
face of an angel" (Acts 6:15).

STEPHEN'S ADDRESS

The stirring address of Stephen, the longest recorded in
Acts, was without question an example of the fulfillment
of the promise of the Lord Jesus given in Matthew 10:19,
20:

"But when they deliver you up, be not anxious how or
what ye shall speak: for it shall be given you in that hour 30
what ye shall speak. For it is not ye that speak, but the
Spirit of your Father that speaketh in you" (A.S.V.).

The Holy Spirit was indeed speaking in Stephen. To these
religionists who claimed to hold so strongly to the law of
Moses and to their ancestral traditions, he rehearsed the

history of the people of Israel from the time the "God of glory appeared" to Abraham (Acts 7:2). He traced the instances of God's grace to them and of their ungracious and ungrateful responses.

As for Moses, who had been so prominently mentioned in their attacks upon Stephen, that great man had been misunderstood and rejected by his people also:

"For he supposed his brethren would have understood how that God by his hand would deliver them: but they
10 understood not. . . . This Moses whom they refused, saying, Who made thee a ruler and a judge? the same did God send to be a ruler and a deliverer by the hand of the angel which appeared to him in the bush" (Acts 7:25, 35).

By referring to Moses' prophecy of the "prophet" (Acts 7:37; compare Deuteronomy 18:15-18), Stephen drew by implication a parallel between Moses and the Lord Jesus Christ. They were opposing Christ because of their supposed respect for and obedience to Moses, but their ancestors had treated Moses the same way:

20 "To whom our fathers would not obey, but thrust him from them, and in their hearts turned back again into Egypt" (Acts 7:39).

This is gathered up in the climactic charge:

"Ye stiffnecked and uncircumcised in heart and ears, ye do always resist the Holy Ghost: as your fathers did, so do ye. Which of the prophets have not your fathers persecuted? and they have slain them which showed before of the coming of the Just One; of whom ye have been now the betrayers and murderers: who have received the law by the disposition
30 of angels, and have not kept it" (Acts 7:51-53).

MARTYRDOM AND PERSECUTION

The fury of these religious leaders is almost unbelievable and indescribable. Like a pack of mad dogs they "gnashed on him with their teeth" (Acts 7:54). Stephen, the faithful witness, filled with the Holy Spirit, was permitted to see his ascended Lord, ready to receive him into His presence. The council, which should have been a solemn, deliberative body,

35

weighing evidence carefully and deciding cases righteously, proved to be instead a cruel, unreasoning, murdering mob.

It is in this scene, so full of pathos and yet so graced by the presence of the Lord, and so ennobled by the forgiving prayer of the martyr, that there first comes into our view the man who—by God's appointment—is largely to fill the succeeding record:

" . . . The witnesses laid down their clothes at a young man's feet, whose name was Saul" (Acts 7:58).

Later, with sorrow, this man was to think back upon this time: 10

"And I said, Lord, they know that I imprisoned and beat in every synagogue them that believed on thee: and when the blood of thy martyr Stephen was shed, I also was standing by, and consenting unto his death, and kept the raiment of them that slew him" (Acts 22:19, 20).

Not yet was any sorrow evident, however, for Saul thought that he was performing service to God (compare the prediction of the Lord Jesus in John 16:2). He continued without compunction on his course of making "havoc 20 of the church" (Acts 8:3).

As occurred many times later in the history of the church, the persecution which arose, because it scattered the believers, only prospered in the end the spread of the gospel (Acts 8:4).

MINISTRY OF PHILIP AND OTHERS IN SAMARIA

Another one of the seven deacons now comes into prominence. Up to this time the gospel had been preached in Jerusalem and presumably to some extent in "all Judea"; now the next part of the Lord's program was to be carried 30 out. Philip's preaching in Samaria was blessed by God and resulted in abounding joy to a multitude of people (Acts 8:5-8).

The question has often been raised concerning the necessity of the laying on of the apostles' hands for the gift of the Holy Spirit. The Holy Spirit had fallen upon the believers in Jerusalem, including the apostles, without the laying on of hands. It seems that in these transition events God was using the apostles, who had been eyewitnesses of the ministry of Christ, to confirm what the Lord Jesus had said about the opening of the kingdom of heaven. These heretofore despised Samaritans were the recipients of the Holy Spirit just as the believing Jews had been; Peter and John attested the opening of the door to them.

The experience of Simon the sorcerer is somewhat difficult to interpret. It may be that he had only an outward profes-
10 sion, not the inner reality of faith. Those who understand Acts 8:13 to mean that Simon had been saved, believe that Peter in admonishing him later was not saying that he was lost, but that he had need of repentance and restoration to fellowship with God. We cannot be sure how deep or how genuine Simon's plea was:

"Pray ye to the Lord for me, that none of these things which ye have spoken come upon me" (Acts 8:24).

The lesson for us is clear, that spiritual gifts are not obtained by fleshly or material means.

20 **ON THE GAZA ROAD**

Men would ordinarily think that while great revival was going on in Samaria it would be foolish for Philip to leave this scene of activity and go out to a lonely road. Here was a man, however, who was sensitive to the leading of the Holy Spirit. Because he was willing to obey, his mission was successful. The witness to one man no doubt was indirectly the cause of winning many others to the Lord Jesus Christ.

We can imagine the perplexity of the Ethiopian official, who was evidently a proselyte to the Jewish religion, as he
30 read the prophecy of Isaiah concerning the sheep brought to the slaughter (Isaiah 53:7, 8). This passage, written by inspiration about seven hundred years before, pictured graphically the vicarious sufferings and death of the Lord Jesus Christ. To the Ethiopian's question about the subject of the prophecy, "Philip opened his mouth . . . and preached unto him Jesus" (Acts 8:35).

37

The Holy Spirit had a prepared listener for a prepared messenger. The response of the Ethiopian to the Word of God was saving faith in the Lord Jesus Christ. The result was great joy. As the newly born-again Ethiopian "went on his way rejoicing" (Acts 8:39), Philip was caught away by the Spirit of God for further intensive and fruitful ministry.

It may well be that some who are studying this course have never received the One about whom the Ethiopian inquired. If you are such a one, may you turn to Him who was *10* wounded for your transgressions and bruised for your iniquities (see Isaiah 53:5).

"All we like sheep have gone astray; we have turned every one to his own way; and the LORD hath laid on him the iniquity of us all" (Isaiah 53:6).

Apply the SQ3R formula to your study using these questions.

1. What were the qualifications of a deacon in the early church?

   _____

2. What was the charge brought against Stephen by the Sanhedrin?

   _____

3. How did Stephen refute the charges of the Sanhedrin?

   _____

4. Who assisted in Stephen's martyrdom but afterward became a famous apostle?

   _____

5. Which of the other deacons became prominent in the early history of the church, and how?

   _____

6. What steps led to the conversion of the Ethiopian eunuch?

   _____

The Conversion of Saul

Ships of the desert.
Israel Gov't Tourist Office, Chicago

YOUR STUDY GUIDE

1. Read the assigned Scripture portion.

2. Take the self-check test based on the Scripture portion.

3. Study the lesson using SQ3R:
   a. Survey the lesson.
   b. Read the SQ3R questions at the end of the lesson.
   c. Read the lesson.
   d. Recite the lesson making marginal notations.
   e. Review the lesson by answering the SQ3R questions boxed in at the end of the lesson.

4. Take the exam.

SCRIPTURE PORTION FOR STUDY

Read Acts 9 twice and then take the following self-check test. Look up the answers to questions in the answer key on page 147.

SELF-CHECK TEST 4

In the right-hand margin check (√) the following statements "True" or "False" based on your reading of the assigned Scripture portion.

		T	F
1.	Saul was converted on his way to Damascus where he planned to persecute the church.	✓	
2.	When He appeared to Saul on the Damascus road, the Lord asked Saul why he was persecuting Him.	✓	
3.	Saul's first desire upon his conversion was to know the Lord's will for his life. 9:6	✓	✓
4.	When Ananias heard that Saul had been saved, he believed the news at once.		✓
5.	The first word by which Ananias addressed Saul when he met him was "brother."	✓	
6.	Because of his bold witness for Christ, the Jews sought to kill Saul.	✓	
7.	The Jerusalem church welcomed Saul with open arms when he went back home.		✓
8.	The conversion of Saul gave the churches a period of rest from persecution. 9:31 ✓	✓	✓
9.	When Peter came to Joppa, he raised a woman named Dorcas from the dead.	✓	
10.	At Joppa, Peter lodged with a man named Simon who was a tanner by trade.	✓	

42

The Conversion of Saul

ACTS 9

This lesson considers the conversion of Saul as recorded for the first time in Acts 9. However, since Paul repeats this story twice more in Acts, you should read chapters 22 and 26 also, and Galatians 1 as well. Note how the various accounts supplement each other.

10 As we have seen, the young man named Saul (who is better known to most of us as the Apostle Paul) first appears in Acts at the scene of Stephen's martyrdom (Acts 7:58). He had been in favor of stoning Stephen to death (Acts 8:1). The thrilling story of how this misguided zealot, "breathing out threatenings and slaughter against the disciples of the Lord" (Acts 9:1), became the pre-eminent preacher of "the faith which once he destroyed" (Galatians 1:23), is an effective evidence of the power of God and of the truth of all the claims of the Lord Jesus Christ.

THE MISSION TO DAMASCUS

20 The man who was later to become the greatest missionary of the Lord Jesus Christ was at this time on a mission of Satan. Saul of Tarsus is perhaps the outstanding example of the fact that sincerity is not enough. He was full of zeal for what he thought was God's cause, but he was utterly wrong. How the Lord Jesus arrested him on his evil course and turned him in an abrupt about-face is the subject of our present study.

Even those Jews who lived in distant places considered themselves in religious matters to be under the jurisdiction

43

of the Sanhedrin in Jerusalem. The extent of Saul's hatred
of the gospel of Christ is seen by his determination to make
the long trip to Damascus for the express purpose of per-
secuting those who were the "disciples of the Lord" (Acts
9:1).

A LIGHT FROM HEAVEN

The light that shone from heaven upon Saul was the appearance of the glory of the risen Lord Jesus. In his defense
before Agrippa, Paul indicated that the time of day was
noon and described the light as being "above the brightness *10*
of the sun" (Acts 26:13). It was no wonder that he was
blinded by it.

The question which he heard from heaven suddenly and
dramatically revealed the enormity of the crime that he had
been committing:

"Saul, Saul, why persecutest thou me?" (Acts 9:4).

Every believer in the Lord Jesus Christ is a member of
His body, vitally related to Him, the Head. Any harm done
to the least member is harm done to Christ. This truth now
broke upon the heart of the stricken persecutor as he heard *20*
the further words, "I am Jesus whom thou persecutest"
(Acts 9:5).

Paul emphatically states that this was an objective appearance of the Lord Jesus Christ, not a subjective vision
(see I Corinthians 9:1; 15:5-8; Galatians 1:11, 12). He
based his claim to apostleship on the fact that he had seen
the risen Lord just as really and objectively as the eleven
had seen Him after His resurrection, and had been directly
commissioned by Him.

On the surface of the English version there seems to be a *30*
discrepancy in the accounts. The first record tells us that
the men accompanying Saul heard a voice (Acts 9:7). In
his recital of this experience many years later to the mob
in Jerusalem, Paul said:

"And they that were with me saw indeed the light, and
were afraid; but they heard not the voice of him that spake
to me" (Acts 22:9).

44

The forms of expression in the original language make the meaning clear. The terms used in the first account inform us that the men with Paul heard the *sound* of the voice; the other record indicates that they did not hear this sound as *words*. In this respect they were like those people who heard the voice of God during the earthly ministry of the Lord Jesus, and who said "that it thundered" (John 12:29).

Paul is an example of one who surrendered his life to the
10 Lord Jesus the moment he believed in Him. This is not always true of believers. Some, because of lack of understanding, incomplete teaching, or some other reason, do not enter into the truth of the yielded life until some time after their acceptance of Christ. To such believers Paul addresses this word of exhortation:

"I beseech you therefore, brethren, by the mercies of God, that ye present your bodies a living sacrifice, holy, acceptable unto God, which is your reasonable service" (Romans 12:1).

20 He himself, the moment that he recognized the Lord Jesus, not only believed on Him, but turned over his life to Him, saying, "Lord, what wilt thou have me to do?" (Acts 9:6).

THE VISIT OF ANANIAS

Here is another Ananias, quite different from the one encountered previously. God breaks down the opposition of His godly servant who protests His command to visit Saul. What grace is manifested! "I have heard . . . how much evil he hath done," Ananias remonstrates with God (Acts 9:13). "He is a chosen vessel unto me," replies the Lord, "to bear
30 my name before the Gentiles, and kings, and the children of Israel" (Acts 9:15).

When Ananias, so instructed by the Lord, finds the man at the house of Judas on Straight Street, he greets him without hesitation as "Brother Saul" (Acts 9:17). God had prepared Saul to receive the visitor, even revealing Ananias' name to him. In his address to the crowd in Jerusalem Paul recounts what Ananias said to him:

45

"And he said, The God of our fathers hath chosen thee, that thou shouldest know his will, and see that Just One, and shouldest hear the voice of his mouth. For thou shalt be his witness unto all men of what thou hast seen and heard . . ." (Acts 22:14, 15).

In a still later account Paul summed up his whole response to all that the Lord had done for him in these words:

"Whereupon, O king Agrippa, I was not disobedient unto the heavenly vision" (Acts 26:19).

PREACHING AND CONSEQUENT PERIL IN DAMASCUS AND JERUSALEM 10

The new believer in the Lord Jesus Christ did not lose time. "Straightway he preached Christ in the synagogues, that he is the Son of God" (Acts 9:20). Well might his hearers be amazed. They knew of his original intent in coming to their city.

Now, of course, as might be expected, the chief persecutor became the persecuted. He confounded his listeners, as Stephen had done, "proving that this is very Christ" (Acts 9:22). Consequently be became the object of a murderous plot; but with the help of other believers he made a thrilling escape from Damascus, being let "down by the wall in a basket" (Acts 9:25). Perhaps as he descended he may have remembered Rahab and the spies (Joshua 2:15) or David's escape with Michal's help (I Samuel 19:12). He gave additional information about this escape in writing to the Corinthians:

"In Damascus the governor under Aretas the king kept the city of the Damascenes with a garrison, desirous to apprehend me: and through a window in a basket was I let down by the wall, and escaped his hands" (II Corinthians 11:32, 33).

The stay in Arabia, mentioned by Paul in Galatians 1:17, evidently took place during the time mentioned in Acts 9:22, 23. The expression "many days" is certainly sufficient to cover it. Paul did not say that he was in Arabia for three years, but that three years elapsed between the time of his

conversion and his return to Jerusalem (Galatians 1:18)
During that time he preached in Damascus, went away to
Arabia, returned to Damascus and preached again, and then
escaped from Damascus.

When Saul returned to Jerusalem he had a new problem
(Acts 9:26). He tried, naturally, to have fellowship with
the believers in Christ. It is not surprising that they were
afraid of him, for he had fully earned the reputation of
being their greatest enemy. But Barnabas, the kindly "son
10 of consolation," as the apostles had named him (Acts 4:36),
came to his aid and vouched for him to the company of
believers.

Saul was not safe in Jerusalem any more than he had
been in Damascus. When it became known that he was the
object of an assassination plot, the believers enabled him
to get away from Jerusalem. From Caesarea on the coast
he departed for Tarsus, his native city in the province of
Cilicia in Asia Minor. There he evidently remained for some
time.

20 Now that the one who had been the chief persecutor had
become a believer in Christ, there ensued a period of relaxa-
tion of persecution. Great blessing resulted.

PETER'S MINISTRY IN LYDDA AND JOPPA

Before the record shifts almost exclusively to the journeys
and ministry of the Apostle Paul, Luke gives a further section on the work of Peter. Part of this will occupy us in
the next lesson. Here at the end of chapter 9 we read of
Peter's visit to Lydda and Joppa, and of two miracles which
God performed through him in those cities.

30 The truth is brought out repeatedly in the Scripture that
the miracles recorded were performed primarily to authen-
ticate the message that was preached. It was not Peter who
had the power to heal Aeneas. "Jesus Christ maketh thee
whole " (Acts 9:34). The result was marvelous:

"And all that dwelt at Lydda and Saron saw him, and
turned to the Lord" (Acts 9:35).

47

The even more notable miracle of the raising of Dorcas (or Tabitha) at Joppa had a similar result:

"And it was known throughout all Joppa; and many believed in the Lord" (Acts 9:42).

Since the completion of the Scriptures God has not desired nor needed to continue performing the same types of miracles over and over again. The message has been authenticated. God's Word is its own best evidence. It comes to each of us and makes its appeal, and we must decide.

Have you decided for the Lord Jesus Christ? Have you *10* received Him as your Saviour? The same Holy Spirit who gives power to believers to live and witness for the Lord Jesus brings conviction through the Word to the hearts of those who do not know the Lord. The Lord Jesus said concerning Him:

"And when he [that is, the Holy Spirit] is come, he will reprove [convict] the world of sin, and of righteousness, and of judgment: of sin, because they believe not on me; of righteousness, because I go to my Father, and ye see me no more; of judgment, because the prince of this world is *20* judged" (John 16:8-11).

Give heed to the Spirit of God as He points you to the Word of God, and accept the Lord Jesus Christ who died for you and rose again. Then like Saul, born from above, you can ask, "Lord, what wilt thou have me to do?"

SQ3R LESSON 4

Questions to use when applying the SQ3R formula.

1. Why was Saul of Tarsus journeying to Damascus?

   _____

2. What supernatural phenomena accompanied Saul's conversion and what is the problem we face in the reporting of these phenomena?

   _____

3. What were the steps in the conversion of Saul?

   _____

4. In what ways were the cities of Damascus and Jerusalem unsafe for Paul after his conversion?

   _____

5. What miracles did Peter perform and what is their significance?

   _____

Peter and the Gentiles

Joppa from the house of Simon the Tanner.

Perry Pictures

YOUR STUDY GUIDE

1. Read the assigned Scripture portion.

2. Take the self-check test based on the Scripture portion.

3. Study the lesson using SQ3R:
   a. Survey the lesson.
   b. Read the SQ3R questions at the end of the lesson.
   c. Read the lesson.
   d. Recite the lesson making marginal notations.
   e. Review the lesson by answering the SQ3R questions boxed in at the end of the lesson.

4. Take the exam.

SCRIPTURE PORTION FOR STUDY

Read Acts 10, 11 and 12 twice and then take the following self-check test. Look up the answers to questions in the answer key on page 147.

55

SELF-CHECK TEST 5

In the right-hand margin check (√) the following statements "True" or "False" based on your reading of the assigned Scripture portion.

		T	F
1.	Cornelius lived at Antioch.		√
2.	Peter's thrice-repeated vision was followed by the visit of three Gentiles to his lodging.	√	
3.	When Cornelius and his household believed on Christ, a kind of second Pentecost took place.	√	
4.	The believers at Jerusalem were thrilled the moment they heard about the inclusion of Gentiles into the church.		√
5.	The believers who were scattered abroad by persecution were careful not to stir up any more trouble by continuing to preach the gospel.		√
6.	The disciples were first called Christians at Antioch.	√	
7.	The Jerusalem church sent Barnabas to Antioch to inquire into the phenomenal growth of the church in that city.	√	
8.	When Barnabas came to Antioch, he decided that Saul's ministry could be effective there.	√	
9.	Herod's plot to kill Peter was foiled by angelic intervention.	√	
10.	The saints at Jerusalem who were praying for Peter's release were expecting that their prayers would be answered.		√

56

Peter and the Gentiles

ACTS 10—12

Up to this point the gospel of Christ had gone out only to Jews and Samaritans. Although the Old Testament foretold the salvation of Gentiles, and the Lord Jesus had commanded the disciples to be His witnesses to the ends of the earth, the truth had not yet dawned upon the Jewish believers that Jew and Gentile were to be one in Christ. Paul
10 explains in Ephesians that this was a "mystery," something not previously revealed, but made known through the apostles (Ephesians 3:1-7).

Now God uses Peter, to whom the Lord Jesus had given "the keys of the kingdom of heaven" (Matthew 16:19), to open the door to the Gentiles also. For most of us this is one of the most important events in Scripture. Before Christ came, the position of the Gentiles was a hopeless one indeed (see Ephesians 2:11, 12). Peter learned, through the experience that God gave him on the housetop, that "God is
20 no respecter of persons: but in every nation he that feareth him, and worketh righteousness, is accepted with him" (Acts 10:34, 35).

GOD'S PREPARATION OF CORNELIUS

In the record of Peter and Cornelius we see clearly the need of all men for the gospel. Some might think that Cornelius was already a saved man, but the Scripture indicates otherwise (see specifically Acts 11:14). The Spirit of God had undoubtedly effected a preparatory work in his heart, but this did not constitute salvation. There is an instructive

57

word for us in the way in which God brought the gospel to this Roman centurion. Why did not the angel tell Cornelius how to be saved? Because God in His sovereign grace has committed the message of the gospel to redeemed human beings, not to angels. What a responsibility this places upon us, and what a privilege! The angel told him to send for a *man* who would give the message.

Are the heathen lost? Yes, they most certainly are. The Word of God is plain (see, for example, Romans 1:18-32). There is no salvation apart from the Lord Jesus Christ. But God in grace can send a messenger. The Holy Spirit through Paul asks a series of searching questions:

"How then shall they call on him in whom they have not believed? and how shall they believe in him of whom they have not heard? and how shall they hear without a preacher? and how shall they preach, except they be sent?" (Romans 10:14, 15).

Peter became the first of a long line of messengers to take the gospel of Christ to the Gentiles. May we do our part to get the message out both to Jew and Gentile.

GOD'S PREPARATION OF PETER

Not only did God have to prepare Cornelius to receive the message, but He had to prepare Peter to give it. While the servants from Cornelius were on their way from Caesarea, approaching Joppa where Peter was staying, God through a vision taught Peter that in Christ the distinction between Jew and Gentile has been removed. This went counter to all Peter's previous training and experience. His reply to God's command is self-contradictory: "Not so, Lord" (Acts 10:14). If I say "No" to Him, is He my *Lord*?

Three times God gave Peter the vision, and then supplied the interpretation by the arrival of the men from Caesarea. On the next day, accompanied by six Jewish believers (Acts 11:12), Peter started with them for Caesarea and Cornelius' house.

58

PETER IN THE HOUSE OF CORNELIUS

Entering into the home of a Gentile for the first time in his
life, Peter proved that he understood the object lesson God
had given him. He preached the gospel to Cornelius and his
friends in the power of the Holy Spirit. "God hath showed
me," he explained, "that I should not call any man common
or unclean" (Acts 10:28). The "middle wall of partition"
had been broken down by the Lord Jesus Christ through His
death on the cross (Ephesians 2:14).

10   Cornelius had assembled a ready congregation to hear
the apostle's message. He expressed their eagerness by
saying:

"Now therefore are we all here present before God, to
hear all things that are commanded thee of God" (Acts
10:33).

Peter's sermon clearly set forth Christ in His death and
resurrection. He showed how he and others were witnesses
both in the sense that they had seen what had taken place
and in the sense that they told what they had seen. This
20   witness of the believers was a corroboration of the witness
of the Old Testament Scriptures:

"To him give all the prophets witness, that through his
name whosoever believeth in him shall receive remission of
sins" (Acts 10:43).

The outpouring of the Holy Spirit was the proof from
God that the faith and experience of Cornelius and the
others with him were genuine. This caused the Jewish believers who had come with Peter to marvel, but Peter had
learned his lesson well. He knew that the Gentiles had re-
30   ceived the same salvation through faith in the Lord Jesus
Christ that he and the other Jewish believers had received.

PETER'S DEFENSE AT JERUSALEM

Word of Peter's preaching to Gentiles came to Jerusalem
and caused some to attack him and question his actions. In
reply, Peter rehearsed the experience God had given him on
the housetop, his summons by Cornelius, and God's gift of

the Holy Spirit to the Gentile believers. He linked this up with what he remembered of the promise of the Lord Jesus:

"Then remembered I the word of the Lord, how that he said, John indeed baptized with water; but ye shall be baptized with the Holy Ghost" (Acts 11:16).

Only the manifest power of God could convince the Jewish believers and overcome their prejudice. Finally they admitted that God was willing to save Gentiles as well as Jews.

CHRISTIANS AT ANTIOCH

The record takes us back in thought to the time of Stephen's 10 martyrdom and indicates how the persecution at that time had caused believers to be scattered into many new places. Wherever they went they had witnessed to the saving power of Christ, but confined their testimony to their fellow Jews. At Antioch in Syria, however, some began to preach to the Gentiles also. Although the Authorized Version reads "Grecians," that is, Hellenists or Greek-speaking Jews, some manuscripts read "Greeks," that is, Gentiles. The latter reading is probably the correct one (Acts 11:20).

Hearing of these developments, the church in Jerusalem 20 sent Barnabas to Antioch. God so mightily used this kindly man that he felt the need to summon help for the task. Consequently he traveled to Tarsus to get Saul, who apparently for some time had been living quietly in his native city, preparing for whatever ministry God had for him. These two friends then carried on a joint Bible-teaching ministry in Antioch for a year. It was in this city that the name *Christians* was first given to the believers—"little Christs," or "followers of Christ." Some interpreters believe the name may have been given at first in derision, but it became 30 an honorable name. Any Christian should feel honored to be so identified with his Lord.

PERSECUTION AGAIN IN JERUSALEM

The prophecy given through Agabus of the coming of famine caused the believers in Antioch to send relief to the believers in Judea. Barnabas and Saul were the agents to carry out this benevolent project of the Antioch church (Acts 11:27-30).

About this time persecution arose again. The Herod mentioned in this passage (Acts 12:1) was. Herod Agrippa I, a grandson of Herod the Great who had been reigning when the Lord Jesus was born, and a nephew of Herod Antipas who reigned over Galilee at the time of the crucifixion. Herod Agrippa I was the father of Herod Agrippa II, the Agrippa mentioned later in this book (Acts 25:13).

10 Herod's cruelty toward the church included his killing of James the son of Zebedee, the brother of John, and his imprisonment of Peter. No doubt he expected that when he brought Peter before the people after the Passover (Acts 12:4), he too would be killed.

The experience of Peter in being delivered from prison is a wonderful evidence of the power of prayer (Acts 12:5). It is also a clear, if ironic, evidence of the unbelief of the human heart. Although the church had been praying constantly for his deliverance, they were slow to believe that 20 God had answered their prayer. The Christians assembled at the home of Mary, the mother of John Mark, were like many of us. They called Rhoda crazy when she excitedly told them that Peter was at the door (Acts 12:15). "Yes, Lord, we're asking You to do this, but we don't really believe You can!" We need to lay hold of God in faith and to keep on believing. It is not that our prayer is powerful or great, but that we are asking a great and powerful God who is able.

We read that "there was no small stir among the soldiers" 30 (Acts 12:18) the next morning. When God is working in and through and for His people there will be a stir. Our lives are so often humdrum because we hinder the work of God by our disobedience and unbelief. It is the life yielded to God that knows the really thrilling adventures in the best sense of the term.

Like so many before and after him, Herod Agrippa I thought of himself more highly than he ought to think. God's judgment fell upon him, as it always does sooner or later (Acts 12:20-23).

The Word of God, however, could not be restrained in its working. It "grew and multiplied" (Acts 12:24). The chapter closes and the transition is made to the second main division of the book by the brief notation of the return of Barnabas and Saul from Jerusalem to Antioch and of their taking John Mark along with them.

SQ3R   LESSON 5

1. What is the "mystery" in which Peter played a part?

   that the gospel should be preached to Gentiles

2. How did God prepare Cornelius for the gospel?

   By an angel

3. How did God prepare Peter to fellowship with the Gentiles?

   a vision

4. On what grounds did Peter defend his communion with the Gentiles to his Jewish critics in Jerusalem?

   _____

5. What city became the first great Gentile center of Christianity?

   _____

6. Why and how did Herod persecute the church at Jerusalem?

   _____

Paul's First Missionary Journey

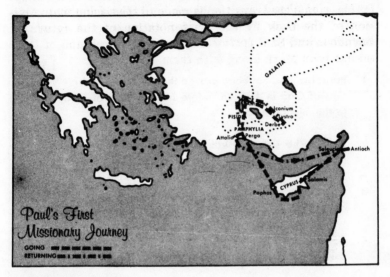

GALATIA

PISID... · Iconium · Lystra
PAMPHYLIA · Derbe
Attalia · Perga

Seleucia · Antioch

Paphos · CYPRUS · Salamis

Paul's First
Missionary Journey

GOING
RETURNING

YOUR STUDY GUIDE

1. Read the assigned Scripture portion.

2. Take the self-check test based on the Scripture portion.

3. Study the lesson using SQ3R:
   a. Survey the lesson.
   b. Read the SQ3R questions at the end of the lesson.
   c. Read the lesson.
   d. Recite the lesson making marginal notations.
   e. Review the lesson by answering the SQ3R questions boxed in at the end of the lesson.

4. Take the exam.

SCRIPTURE PORTION FOR STUDY

Read Acts 13 and 14 twice and then take the following self-check test. Look up the answers to questions in the answer key on page 147.

SELF-CHECK TEST 6

In the right-hand margin check (√) the following statements "True" or "False" based on your reading of the assigned Scripture portion.

	T	F
1. Barnabas and Saul had proved themselves able servants of God in Antioch before being called of God to the mission field.	√	
2. Elymas the sorcerer was converted through Paul's preaching on Cyprus.		√
3. At Antioch in Pisidia, Paul formulated the policy of going to the Gentiles first with the gospel.		√
4. The Jews were envious at the numbers of Gentiles converted through Paul's preaching.	√	
5. When they were persecuted at Antioch in Pisidia, Paul and Barnabas shook off the dust of their feet as a testimony against the Jews there.	√	
6. The Jews were again ringleaders in persecuting the missionaries at Iconium and Lystra.	√	
7. At Lystra Paul healed a man who had been lame from birth.	√	
8. The pagans at Lystra wanted to worship Paul and Barnabas as gods.	√	
9. Paul and Barnabas decided that it would be safest to return to Antioch in Syria by a different route, so carefully avoided going back to the cities where they had been persecuted.		√
10. Arriving back at Antioch in Syria, the missionaries were too restless to stay there for long.		√

Paul's First Missionary Journey

ACTS 13, 14

From Acts 13 on, Saul, or Paul as he now comes to be known, who has already been introduced in the record, becomes the dominant character in the book. He tells the Corinthians later how he engaged in "journeyings often" (II Corinthians 11:26). The magnificent Roman roads, unparalleled up to that time, connecting all parts of the empire, 10 and the freedom of the Mediterranean Sea from pirates, accomplished some time before by Roman naval power, were used by God, along with other means, for the spread of the gospel of Christ. Paul and his companions were untiring in their travels because they had a divine commission and were constrained by the love of the Lord Jesus Christ Himself (see II Corinthians 5:14-21).

THE IMPORTANCE OF ANTIOCH

The book of Acts contains the record of three great missionary journeys of Paul, followed by the voyage to Rome. 20 In this second part of the book Antioch in Syria, rather than Jerusalem, becomes the center of Christian activity. It was here, as we have seen, that the name *Christians* had first been applied to the believers. Each of Paul's missionary journeys began at Antioch, and each ended there, except the third. On that journey he was arrested in Jerusalem and was unable to return and report to the home church.

The first missionary journey covered the island of Cyprus, the native land of Barnabas, and a number of cities in the southern part of Asia Minor.

65

THE MISSIONARY CALL

Among the leaders of the church at Antioch were Barnabas
(mentioned first) and Saul (mentioned last) (Acts 13:1).
God called these two men to a special task. It is interesting
to observe that in the beginning the record speaks of Barnabas and Saul, but later of Paul and Barnabas. God in His
sovereign purpose was bringing the apostle to the Gentiles
to the fore. Earlier, it will be remembered, the Lord Jesus
had said that He would send Paul to distant places among
the Gentiles (Acts 9:15; compare 22:21). Notice that God   *10*
sent these men forth, while at the same time the church sent
them (Acts 13:3, 4). The verb used of the believers means
literally, "they let them go." In the sending forth of a true
missionary God Himself must be the sender. The church's
part is to recognize the call of God and to consent to His will.

ADVENTURES IN CYPRUS

Sailing from Seleucia, the port of Antioch, Barnabas and
Saul went first to the island of Cyprus. John Mark, who was
a relative of Barnabas (Colossians 4:10), went with them
as a helper.   *20*

At Paphos, on the island of Cyprus, the name *Paul* is first
used in the record for Saul of Tarsus (Acts 13:9). Some
believe that he took the name for the first time here, possibly
because of the Roman proconsul, Sergius Paulus, who became a believer (Acts 13:12). It is more likely, however,
that the apostle had both names from childhood, Saul being
his Hebrew name (as a namesake of the first king of Israel,
who was also from the tribe of Benjamin), and Paul being
his Roman name, since as a native of Tarsus he was a Roman citizen from birth. Now that his ministry was to be   *30*
primarily among the Gentiles in various parts of the Roman
Empire, he made use exclusively of his Roman name. It is
probable also that the other name, Saul, which he had used
during his Hebrew period, would have unhappy connotations
for him, because under that name he had persecuted the
church of God.

Here it becomes evident that Paul was the chief speaker, as is mentioned later in the history (Acts 14:12). There is no indication that Barnabas was envious of Paul for his assumption of the leadership. Some in Barnabas' position would have remonstrated that they should have the leadership by right of priority in time, and also by virtue of all that had been done to help the newer Christian. In this regard Barnabas demonstrated the Holy Spirit's assessment of him. He was a kindly, benevolent man (Acts 11:24), who
10 put the will of God first and accepted the place God assigned to him without envy or rancor. His later disagreement with Paul does not negate this.

In his rebuke of the sorcerer Bar-jesus (Elymas) and the accompanying miracle of judgment (Acts 13:9-11), Paul asserted his apostolic authority which he had received from the risen Lord, and attested his message.

AT PISIDIAN ANTIOCH

At Perga on the southern coast of what we call Asia Minor, John Mark turned back and returned to his home in Jeru-
20 salem. We are not told his specific reason. This incident was to cause dissension later between Paul and Barnabas.

Many Bible students do not realize, at least at first, that Asia Minor in Paul's day was a center of Greco-Roman civilization. There were many populous and wealthy cities there. For some reason we almost always associate the term *pioneer missionary* with jungles and remote semipopulated areas, but Paul was a true pioneer missionary in the sense that he brought the gospel where it had never been preached before. His strategy, under the direction of the Holy Spirit,
30 was to touch some of the great centers of civilization from which the gospel could then radiate to outlying districts as the spokes from the hub of a wheel.

It was Paul's custom as he visited various cities to preach first in the Jewish synagogue. The rulers of the synagogues ordinarily extended opportunities of speaking to visitors who seemed to be teachers. At Pisidian Antioch, being given this courtesy, Paul, with a gesture that seems to have been characteristic of him, connected the gospel with the history of Israel. In this he seems to have been following a pattern somewhat like that of Stephen.

Paul showed the relationship of the Lord Jesus to David and to the covenant that God had made with David, and further pointed out how David by inspiration had prophesied the resurrection of the Lord Jesus Christ from the dead. He went on to say:

"Be it known unto you therefore, men and brethren, that through this man is preached unto you the forgiveness of 10 sins: and by him all that believe are justified from all things, from which ye could not be justified by the law of Moses" (Acts 13:38, 39).

The message at first found a ready response from many. The next week a vast crowd came together to hear the preaching of the gospel. By this time the enemy had gathered his forces. Contradiction and blasphemy met the preachers and their message. Consequently Paul and Barnabas turned to the Gentiles. What rejoicing there was among those who were privileged to hear the good news of salvation 20 for the first time! The Word of God was "published throughout all the region" (Acts 13:49).

WORSHIPED AND STONED

The messengers went from place to place, following the instruction of the Lord Jesus that when they were persecuted in one city they were to flee to another (Matthew 10:23). The work went on, in Iconium, in Lystra, and in Derbe. In Iconium they continued a long time (Acts 14:3), until the opposition, led by unbelieving Jews, became so strong that their lives were endangered. Many, both of Jews and 30 Gentiles, were saved through this evangelistic campaign.

In Lystra God forwarded the work by enabling Paul to work a miracle in the healing of a crippled man. This event and its sequel show up the fickleness and instability of humanity. The miracle caused the superstitious pagans to think that Paul and Barnabas were gods who had come down to visit men, as the old Greek and Roman myths often declared. The people identified Barnabas with Zeus (A.V., "Jupiter"), the king of the gods, and Paul with Hermes (A.V., "Mercurius"), because he was the chief spokesman. Hermes was regarded by the Greeks as the messenger of the gods. In spite of all they could say, Paul and Barnabas could scarcely restrain these deluded polytheists from worshiping them. The missionaries exhorted their hearers to turn from these empty superstitions to the true and living God who created all things and sustains all things in His goodness (Acts 14:14-18).

Not long afterward, however, at the instigation of unbelieving Jews from Antioch and Iconium, the people of Lystra stoned Paul, leaving him for dead (Acts 14:19). Such is earthly fame and fortune. Today a god, tomorrow an outcast; today idolized, tomorrow stoned! But if Paul and Barnabas had been seeking earthly fame and fortune they would have turned back long before this; indeed they would not have started out at all. They sought to do God's will at God's command. Because their aim was to please God, they could not be turned from their course either by men's foolish and mistaken worship, or by men's equally mistaken and malicious opposition.

As they retraced their steps from Derbe, through Lystra, Iconium and Antioch, the missionaries showed the importance and value of follow-up. They confirmed "the souls of the disciples," and exhorted "them to continue in the faith" (Acts 14:22). Wherever possible the messengers of God who had first won men to Christ kept in touch with their converts, doing everything they could to assist the young Christians to grow in grace. This is not a denial by any means of God's ability to keep those who have put their trust in Him. It is God's ordained way to build up the body of Christ. We see in other parts of the New Testament how Paul nurtured those whom God had won through him by writing letters to them in which he not only gave them instruction, but reminded them of his constant prayers on their behalf.

BACK HOME AGAIN

The missionaries who had been sent out by the church at Antioch gave a full account of their stewardship on their return. The church which had supported them was privileged to share with them in the results of the work. It was all God's doing and they gave God all the glory (Acts 14:27). Paul and Barnabas then had a long period of ministry at Antioch.

In the book of Acts we can see many principles that should guide us in our individual witnessing and in our *10* corporate missionary effort today. Just as the Lord Jesus Christ, risen from the dead and ascended to heaven, could continue His *acts* through the disciples of the first century, so He can continue His *acts* through you and me if we are willing to yield ourselves to Him and allow His Holy Spirit to act through us.

SQ3R   LESSON 6

1. In what ways did Roman rule expedite the missionary activities of Paul?

_____

2. Where did each of Paul's missionary journeys begin?

_____

3. What can be learned about a call to the mission field from the call of Paul and Barnabas?

_____

4. Why did Saul change his name to Paul?

_____

5. What was Paul's missionary strategy?

_____

6. How was the gospel received on the mainland of Asia Minor?

_____

7. In what way did Paul and Barnabas discharge their obligation to the church at Antioch after their first missionary journey?

_____

The Council of Jerusalem

YOUR STUDY GUIDE

1. Read the assigned Scripture portion.

2. Take the self-check test based on the Scripture portion.

3. Study the lesson using SQ3R:
   a. <u>Survey</u> the lesson.
   b. <u>Read</u> the SQ3R questions at the end of the lesson.
   c. <u>Read</u> the lesson.
   d. <u>Recite</u> the lesson making marginal notations.
   e. <u>Review</u> the lesson by answering the SQ3R questions boxed in at the end of the lesson.

4. Take the exam.

The Via Dolorosa in Jerusalem.
Arab Information Center, N.Y.

SCRIPTURE PORTION FOR STUDY

Read Acts 15 twice and then take the following self-check test. Look up the answers to questions in the answer key on page 147.

SELF-CHECK TEST 7

*In the right-hand margin check (√) the following state-
ments "True" or "False" based on your reading of the
assigned Scripture portion.*

	T	F
1. The Judaizers (those who insisted that all converts be circumcised and keep the law of Moses) came to Antioch from Samaria.		✓
2. The Jerusalem conference was convened to come to some conclusion regarding the claims of the Judaizers.	✓	
3. Some Pharisees in the church insisted that the claims of the Judaizers were right and wanted them enforced.	✓	
4. Peter insisted that the claims of the Judaizers were right and wanted them enforced.		✓
5. Barnabas and Paul told the assembly what God had done through them among the Gentiles.	✓	
6. James, the Lord's brother, who was one of the pillars of the Jerusalem church, insisted that the Gentiles be left alone and not be troubled by the Judaizers.	✓	
7. The elders at the Jerusalem church wrote a letter to the Gentile churches in which they stated the results of the Jerusalem conference.	✓	
8. The believers at Antioch were much displeased at the results of the Jerusalem conference.		✓
9. Those who confirmed the message contained in the letter from the Jerusalem conference were Judas and Silas.	✓	
10. Paul's companion on his second missionary journey was Silas.	✓	

The Council of Jerusalem

ACTS 15

The council of Jerusalem marks a great crisis in the early history of the Christian church, and its decision blazons forth that liberty which Paul so forcefully describes in the Epistle to the Galatians. If the Judaizers had had their way, Christianity would have become just a minor Jewish sect which would have soon withered away. These false teachers
10 could not have their way, of course, for the Lord Jesus Christ had announced that He would build His church, and He had said, "The gates of hell shall not prevail against it" (Matthew 16:18).

A VEXING QUESTION AND ITS ANSWER

The men who came to Antioch from Judea preached an unsettling and disquieting doctrine, insisting that Gentiles had to become Jews in order to be saved. For this reason such teachers are known in history as the Judaizers. This chapter tells of the turmoil in the church from this question, and
20 of the decision concerning the question at the Jerusalem conference.

In the beginning of the preaching of the gospel only Jews had been evangelized. Then God had used Peter to open the door to the Gentiles. Nevertheless, there were still those among the Jews who insisted that Christianity was only a form of Judaism. They taught that a Gentile had to become a Jew, submitting himself to the law and to ordinances in order to be saved (Acts 15:1). One can imagine the consternation in the church at Antioch, made up mostly of
30 Gentiles who had been rejoicing in their salvation through

79

the Lord Jesus Christ, when these men came among them, no doubt claiming authority from the church in Jerusalem.

The record speaks of the vehement "dissension and disputation" which resulted (Acts 15:2). Paul, by the grace of God, was particularly alive to the import of the issue. Christian freedom was at stake, as he indignantly pointed out in his Epistle to the Galatians. If the Gentile believers were to succumb to the blandishments of the Judaizers and submit to Jewish ordinances, they would be making the admission that Christ was not enough, that the Saviour was 10 insufficient for salvation. Paul tells in Galatians how at Jerusalem he resisted the attempts on the part of some to compel Titus, a Gentile Christian, to submit to the ordinance of circumcision. Paul realized as few others did that surrender of such a principle would be fatal to Christian liberty (see Galatians 2:4, 5). He indicates, in the passage referred to, that these Judaizers were "false brethren," not true believers at all.

THE ISSUE BEFORE THE COUNCIL

Because the apostles were in Jerusalem it seemed good to 20 the Christians of Antioch to send a delegation there for consultation. Paul and Barnabas and certain others made the trip. Some at that time, and many in the centuries since, have intimated that there was a cleavage between Paul and the other apostles about this question. This is completely untrue. The cleavage that existed was not between Paul and the Twelve, but between Paul and the Twelve on the one side, and the Judaizers on the other. There was no disagreement among the apostles about the question.

Apparently in the discussion no one was denying that 30 salvation came through the Lord Jesus Christ. The question was—does salvation come through Christ *alone* or through Christ plus something else? This is the great divide in Bible doctrine. This is the test of grace. Paul in Romans shows that grace, in order to be grace, must be *only* grace:

"And if by grace, then is it no more of works: otherwise grace is no more grace. But if it be of works, then is it no more grace: otherwise work is no more work" (Romans 11:6).

Peter testified that God had put no difference between Jews and Gentiles, but had saved both by His grace through faith. He asked why the believers now would want to put a grievous yoke on the Gentile Christians, a yoke, as he pointed out, "which neither our fathers nor we were able to bear" (Acts 15:10).

Peter was not talking theoretically. God through him had
10 offered salvation to the Gentiles. Nor did Paul and Barnabas speak theoretically as they recounted what God had done through them among the Gentiles. God, declared all these men, had given the gift of the Holy Spirit to Gentiles when they believed, without any reference to the law of Moses or to ordinances. Why should these believers now take the backward step of depending upon that which could not avail?

THE DECISION OF THE COUNCIL

James seems to have been presiding at the council. This is
20 "James the Lord's brother" (Galatians 1:19; Matthew 13:55), the writer of the Epistle of James and the brother of Jude. He gave the summation of the evidence in what C. I. Scofield has called the most important passage dispensationally in the New Testament (Scofield Reference Edition of the Bible, page 1169).

What is God's purpose in this age? Is the church Israel, and is Israel the church? These are basic questions that are controverted today even among believers. What James declared is essentially what Paul also teaches in Ephesians
30 3, that the church is a body made up of both Jews and Gentiles, distinct from both, a new entity, not clearly revealed in the Old Testament; in other words, a "mystery" (see Ephesians 3:1-6; compare also I Corinthians 10:32).

The quotation which James made from Amos (compare Amos 9:11, 12 with Acts 15:15-18) has been variously interpreted. Many take it to mean that the salvation of the Gentiles in this age is the fulfillment of the passage in

Amos. Taking the full context into account, however, and James' words of introduction to the quotation, it can be seen that he was showing a sequence of events:

First, the visiting of the Gentiles to take out a people—the church.

Then, the rebuilding of the tabernacle of David—the restoration of Israel.

Then, the winning of the residue of men—the Millennial Age.

This is the only order that agrees with the teaching of other parts of Scripture. To make the passage in Amos refer exclusively to the present Church Age is to do violence to the use which James made of it (see also Romans 11:24-27).

James clearly spoke for the body of believers as opposed to the Judaizers. Paul in his Epistle to the Galatians tells us more about the private conversations of the apostles:

"For they who seemed to be somewhat in conference added nothing to me: but contrariwise, when they saw that the gospel of the uncircumcision was committed unto me, as the gospel of the circumcision was unto Peter . . . and when James, Cephas, and John, who seemed to be pillars, perceived the grace that was given unto me, they gave to me and Barnabas the right hands of fellowship; that we should go unto the heathen [i.e., the Gentiles], and they unto the circumcision" (Galatians 2:6, 7, 9).

The church recognized that the Gentile believers had no relationship to the law. Even the Jews, who had the law of God, could not be saved by keeping the law. Neither Jew nor Gentile could attain the favor of God by law-keeping. To attempt to force believers under the law, either as a means of justification or as a means of Christian living, was to introduce a different gospel, which was really not a gospel at all, but a terrible perversion of the gospel, as Paul explains (Galatians 1:6-9).

The practices from which the Gentile believers were asked to refrain were those which would give offense. Along with these things was coupled the moral behavior which would adorn the doctrine, that believers might be pure in their lives as well as in their faith.

RESULTS OF THE LETTER

The letter from the church at Jerusalem to the believers in Antioch and the surrounding territories was a cause of great rejoicing among the Gentile believers (Acts 15:31). This was a confirmation of their liberty in Christ. They had weathered the storm of external persecution and had thrived; now they had weathered the storm of internal
10 schism. The word that was given by letter was confirmed orally, not only by Paul and Barnabas, who had been sent to Jerusalem by the Antioch church, but also by the men sent from Jerusalem, Judas Barsabas and Silas (Acts 15:22, 32). The last named remained in Antioch and was to have a prominent part in the later record.

BEGINNING OF THE SECOND MISSIONARY JOURNEY

The idea for the second missionary journey originated with Paul (Acts 15:36). He and Barnabas disagreed about the latter's suggestion that they take Mark with them.
20   Many interpreters seem to feel that they must take sides here; that they must pronounce judgment, declaring that Paul was right, or that Barnabas was right. Human relationships are frequently so complex that we often cannot state who is completely in the right or who is completely in the wrong. God uses all kinds of instruments and makes even the wrath of man, including human disagreements, to praise Him. No doubt Barnabas was inclined to be more forgiving of Mark's former departure from them because the young man was his relative. He apparently saw a poten-
30 tial in him which in his judgment overrode any previous shortcomings. That there was some basis for this is seen in the fact that Mark did later perform admirable service for Christ, including the writing of one of the Gospels. Years later Paul acknowledged Mark's worth (II Timothy 4:11).
    On the other hand, Paul, on the basis of previous experience, had what seemed to him ample justification for doubt-

ing Mark's usefulness. Each had reasons for the disagreement. Who are we to say which was right and which was wrong? A principle that Paul himself enunciated is applicable here:

"Therefore judge nothing before the time, until the Lord come, who both will bring to light the hidden things of darkness, and will make manifest the counsels of the hearts: and then shall every man have praise of God" (I Corinthians 4:5).

This incident is certainly relevant to our time when we *10* see so many different ideas of methods and procedures in the work of the Lord. Each of us must stand by his convictions as he sees things in the light of God's Word, but we must be charitable toward our brethren who have different convictions from ourselves.

God is sovereign in the disposition of His workers. We look upon the disagreement of Paul and Barnabas as a tragedy, but even through this the spread of the gospel was expanded. Instead of one gospel team, there were now two. Barnabas and Mark sailed for Cyprus, while Paul and Silas *20* traveled overland through Syria and Cilicia.

SQ3R LESSON 7

1. What was at stake should the Judaizers gain their way?

   The very freedom we have in Christ!

2. How does Galatians 2 cast light upon the Jerusalem conference recorded in Acts 15?

   The Judaizers were false brethren.

3. How was the Jerusalem church divided on the issue before the conference?

   Paul & the twelve vs. Judaizers

4. How was the issue settled?

   _____

5. In what way did Paul and Barnabas disagree over the proposed second missionary journey?

   whether to take Mark

6. How did God overrule the separation of Paul and Barnabas to the extension of missionary activity?

   sending two teams

Paul's Second Missionary Journey

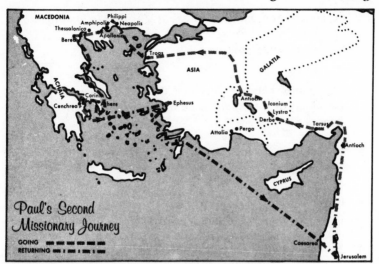

YOUR STUDY GUIDE

1. Read the assigned Scripture portion.

2. Take the self-check test based on the Scripture portion.

3. Study the lesson using SQ3R:
   a. Survey the lesson.
   b. Read the SQ3R questions at the end of the lesson.
   c. Read the lesson.
   d. Recite the lesson making marginal notations.
   e. Review the lesson by answering the SQ3R questions boxed in at the end of the lesson.

4. Take the exam.

SCRIPTURE PORTION FOR STUDY

Read Acts 15:36—18:22 twice and then take the following self-check test. Look up the answers to questions in the answer key on page 147.

SELF-CHECK TEST 8

In the right-hand margin check (√) the following statements "True" or "False" based on your reading of the assigned Scripture portion.

	T	F
1. The quarrel between Paul and Barnabas was over the fitness of John Mark to be a member of the missionary party.	√	
2. Timothy became a member of Paul's missionary team at Lystra.	√	
3. It was at Troas that Paul received the call to evangelize Macedonia.	√	
4. Paul's first convert in Europe was a woman from the Asiatic city of Thyatira.	√	
5. The Philippian jailer committed suicide when he discovered that an earthquake had opened the prison doors and released his prisoners.		√
6. The unbelieving Jews who had persecuted Paul at Thessalonica followed him to Berea to make trouble there also.	√	
7. When Paul preached at Mars Hill in Athens there were hundreds of people saved.		√
8. At Corinth Paul found employment as a tentmaker with Andronicus and Junia.		√
9. The deputy of Achaia was Gallio.	√	
10. When Paul first visited Ephesus, the Jews asked him to leave at once.		√

Paul's Second Missionary Journey

ACTS 15:36—18:22

It is thrilling to see the rapid spread of the gospel in the first century. On Paul's second missionary journey, the gospel entered the continent of Europe. The plan appointed by the Lord Jesus continued on, with the message eventually to reach the ends of the earth. The risen Christ continued to act through His disciples by the power of the Holy Spirit.

10 THE JOURNEY, PLANNED AND UNPLANNED

Paul's intention in starting the second missionary journey was to revisit the places where he had gone on his former journey. In the purpose of God, however, this became greatly expanded and much pioneer territory was entered. We note that the Lord led in this by closing doors as well as by opening doors.

The second missionary journey covered at least two years, for Paul was in Corinth a year and a half (Acts 18:11) as well as briefer periods in a number of other cities. It in-
20 volved a much larger territory than the first journey.

At Lystra, one of the cities of the first journey, Paul and Silas were joined by the young man Timothy, who became a close friend and valuable helper throughout the remainder of the apostle's life. It is probable that Timothy's mother and grandmother (mentioned in II Timothy 1:5) had been saved during Paul's previous visit.

Evidently Paul had desired to enter the province of Asia to preach the gospel, but it was not yet God's time. The workers "were forbidden of the Holy Ghost to preach the
30 word in Asia" (Acts 16:6). Paul's extended ministry in

that province came some years later on his third missionary journey. In whatever way God did it, He kept them in a path toward the northwest coast of Asia Minor, permitting them to turn neither to the left hand nor to the right.

CALL TO MACEDONIA AND THE RESPONSE

At Troas, ancient Troy, Paul received a special call in a vision of a man of Macedonia. Paul's conviction that he should minister in Macedonia was shared by all his associates. They therefore sailed from Troas, "assuredly gathering that the Lord had called us for to preach the gospel unto them" (Acts 16:10).

The emergence of the pronoun "we" at this place shows that Luke, the writer of the book, had joined Paul and his companions at Troas. We know nothing of Luke's background. He is identified in the Scripture as a physician (see Colossians 4:14), and is traditionally thought to have been a Greek, apparently the only Gentile among the New Testament writers.

The first extensive ministry in Europe was in Philippi, a leading city in Macedonia and a Roman colony; that is, it had been settled originally by Roman veterans and their families. Since there were not enough Jews in the city to have a synagogue, worship services were held by devout women at the riverside. Here the merchantwoman Lydia, originally from Thyatira in Asia Minor, heard Paul preach and the Lord opened her heart (Acts 16:14).

TESTIMONY AND IMPRISONMENT

The preaching continued in the city. The miraculous healing of the demon-possessed slave girl brought trouble; Paul and Silas were brought before the magistrates. The charge was exceedingly vague and general, but connected with the inevitable appeal to patriotism. As Paul later pointed out, the whole so-called trial was farcical and illegal. Nevertheless God was working out His purposes.

It is easy to sing praises to God when surroundings are pleasant and life is serene. It is not so easy in prison stocks.

Yet this is what Paul and Silas did. The Holy Spirit lifted them above the circumstances. God's intervention through an earthquake brought fright to the jailer. This was no ordinary earthquake; "all the doors were opened, and every one's bands were loosed" (Acts 16:26). The jailer, who may have heard the message of Paul previously, was brought under strong conviction. "Sirs," he cried, "what must I do to be saved?" The answer was simple and forthright, "Believe on the Lord Jesus Christ, and thou shalt be saved, and
10 thy house" (Acts 16:30, 31).

These people, Lydia and her household, the jailer and his family, and others like them, formed the nucleus of the church at Philippi, which always had a close and friendly relationship with Paul, and to which he addressed his Epistle to the Philippians many years later during his first Roman imprisonment.

We see in this instance one of several occasions in the book of Acts on which Paul used his Roman citizenship which he possessed from birth to good advantage. The
20 magistrates, realizing that they had acted illegally, feared that they would be called to account. Consequently they besought the missionaries to leave before any further trouble could arise (Acts 16:39).

THESSALONICA AND BEREA

Thessalonica, another important city of Macedonia, had a larger Jewish population than Philippi. There Paul and his associates began their ministry in the synagogue. One of the most remarkable results of Paul's stay in Thessalonica was the insight of these people into the things of God. In
30 only one brief visit they were not only won to Christ but also instructed in the depths of Christian teaching indicated in the Epistles to the Thessalonians. Dealing with some of the obscure and difficult details connected with the second coming of Christ, Paul asks, "Remember ye not, that, when I was yet with you, I told you these things?" (II Thessalonians 2:5).

We are too inclined to limit the Holy Spirit, not realizing

how much He can do in the life of a new-born child of God. Paul was able to instruct in the deep things because he was dependent on the Holy Spirit.

As so often in the apostle's travels, he was opposed and persecuted by his own unbelieving race. He explains this later to the Thessalonians:

"For ye, brethren, became followers of the churches of God which in Judea are in Christ Jesus: for ye also suffered like things of your own countrymen, even as they have of the Jews: who both killed the Lord Jesus, and their own *10* prophets, and have persecuted us.; and they please not God, and are contrary to all men: forbidding us to speak to the Gentiles that they might be saved, to fill up their sins alway: for the wrath is come upon them to the uttermost" (I Thessalonians 2:14-16).

Fleeing from Thessalonica, Paul and Silas came to Berea. The statement made about the people in this city has furnished a name and an incentive to innumerable Bible classes since that day:

"These were more noble than those in Thessalonica, in *20* that they received the word with all readiness of mind, and searched the scriptures daily, whether those things were so" (Acts 17:11).

Opposition from Thessalonica led to Paul's having to leave this city also. Apart from his usual traveling companions, he made his way to Athens, the intellectual and cultural center of the Greek world.

DECLARATION OF THE UNKNOWN GOD

Paul, being a highly educated man, was doubtless aware of Greek thought and literature. He probably knew much about *30* the past glories of Athens. But all of this was insignificant compared to its spiritual condition. He was deeply moved as he saw the terrible prevalence of idolatry. These people who made such a fetish of philosophy—the love of wisdom— were so foolish as to bow down before the works of men's hands. The folly of worshiping that which human hands have made constituted Paul's chief indictment of idolatry (see Romans 1:22, 23).

The Athenian intellectuals and dilettantes thought of Paul as a "setter forth of strange gods: because he preached unto them Jesus, and the resurrection" (Acts 17:18). Since many of their deities had names of abstract qualities, they apparently thought that "Resurrection" (Greek *Anastasis,* from another form of which has come the feminine name Anastasia) was a goddess. Paul met these people where
10 they were, building upon their religiosity and the confession of many of them that God was essentially unknown.

Some interpreters of Scripture have argued that Paul made a mistake in the type of address he gave on the Areopagus (Mars Hill); they insist that it was too philosophical. One should be very careful, however, about criticizing the words of an apostle unless there is clear indication in the Scripture that he was out of line with the will of God. This was an instance of becoming all things to all men in order to save some (see I Corinthians 9:22). The fact that the
20 converts seem to have been comparatively few (Acts 17:34) is no proof that the message was wrong.

In his message Paul pointed to God as the Creator and the Judge of the world, and connected these past and future works of God by Christ's resurrection as the proof and guarantee of God's intervention in the world.

THE FIRST CORINTHIAN MINISTRY

From Athens Paul proceeded to Corinth, the capital of the Roman province of Achaia, comprising southern Greece. Corinth was a thriving commercial city. It was there that
30 he became acquainted with Aquila and Priscilla, who became his close friends and fellow laborers in the gospel. Many of the Jews believed in Christ, including Crispus, the ruler of the synagogue. The Lord Jesus Himself encouraged Paul, assuring him that He had many people in this immoral, pagan city (Acts 18:10).

The Jews again stirred up trouble for the apostle. Bringing him before the judgment seat of Gallio, the Roman pro-

consul, they accused him of teaching men contrary to the law. Gallio showed a proper indifference to such questions, recognizing that no Roman law had been broken. This caused some of the Greeks to turn on Sosthenes, who evidently had succeeded Crispus as the leader of the Jewish synagogue. Several years later when Paul wrote his First Epistle to the Corinthians, he joined the name of "Sosthenes our brother" to his own in the salutation. Could this be the same man? Possibly so, for if God could save one synagogue ruler, He could surely save another. The Jews seem to have   10
had difficulty keeping a leader of their synagogue when Paul and the gospel were around!

The second missionary journey drew to a close as Paul left Achaia, stopped briefly in Ephesus with a promise to return later, hurried to Jerusalem and greeted the church there (Acts 18:22), and then returned to his home base at Antioch.

What a fruitful ministry was compressed into those comparatively few months. As we read the letters addressed to some of these churches, we learn something of the earn-   20
estness of purpose of the apostle and his little company. The two epistles to the Thessalonians were written while on this journey, probably during Paul's lengthy stay in Corinth. The two letters to the Corinthians were written later, while Paul was engaged in his third missionary journey. The letter to the Philippians came still later, during the apostle's first Roman imprisonment. In all of them we see his compassionate care for the churches.

SQ3R LESSON 8

1. What parts of Paul's second missionary journey were planned and what parts were unplanned?

   They planned on re-visiting places they had gone. didn't plan to go to Macedonia

2. How did Paul learn that it was God's will for him to go to Europe with the gospel?

   A dream.

3. At what point in Paul's second missionary journey did Luke become a member of the team?

   At Troas

4. Why was Paul imprisoned at Philippi and what were the results? *formal & illegal*

   a vague appeal to patriotism

5. Why were the Bereans "more noble" than the Thessalonicans? *with open minds.*

   they searched scripture daily

6. How did Paul preach to the Athenian intellectuals?

7. What success did Paul have at Corinth?

   Great success —

95

Paul's Third Missionary Journey

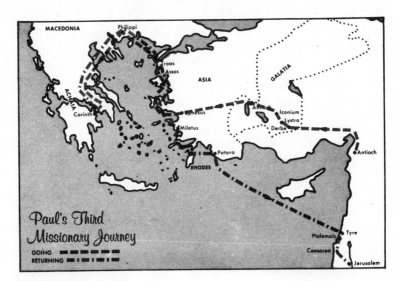

YOUR STUDY GUIDE

> 1. Read the assigned Scripture portion.
>
> 2. Take the self-check test based on the Scripture portion.
>
> 3. Study the lesson using SQ3R:
>   a. Survey the lesson.
>   b. Read the SQ3R questions at the end of the lesson.
>   c. Read the lesson.
>   d. Recite the lesson making marginal notations.
>   e. Review the lesson by answering the SQ3R-questions boxed in at the end of the lesson.
>
> 4. Take the exam.

SCRIPTURE PORTION FOR STUDY

Read Acts 18:23—21:17 twice and then take the following self-check test. Look up the answers to questions in the answer key on page 147.

SELF-CHECK TEST 9

In the right-hand margin check (√) the following statements "True" or "False" based on your reading of the assigned Scripture portion.

	T	F
1. When Apollos came to Ephesus he was shown the truth about the way of God by Aquila and Priscilla.	√	
2. The sons of Sceva were able to cast out evil spirits just as effectively as Paul.		√
3. The converts of Paul in Ephesus made a great bonfire of their unholy books.	√	
4. The riot in Ephesus led by Demetrius resulted in Paul's imprisonment.		√
5. After leaving Ephesus Paul spent three years in Greece.	√	√
6. At Troas Paul raised a man from the dead.	√	
7. Paul could honestly tell the Ephesian elders that he was pure from the blood of all men.	√	
8. Paul assured the elders of the Ephesian church that he would see them again before long.		√
9. Paul received warning that he would run into trouble at Jerusalem.	√	
10. The Jerusalem brethren received Paul and his party gladly.	√	

Paul's Third Missionary Journey

ACTS 18:23—21:17

Each of the great missionary journeys began at Antioch in
Syria. The first and the second ended there as well. The
third, as we are now to see, ended differently. On his way
back to Antioch, Paul visited Jerusalem, as he had done
toward the end of the previous journey; but this time he
was arrested and was unable to return to Antioch. One of
10 the most controversial questions in the book of Acts is
whether Paul should have gone to Jerusalem in view of the
warnings which he received.

AN EVENTFUL TERM OF MISSIONARY SERVICE

Paul's third missionary journey was even more eventful
than those that had preceded. During this journey he had a
long sojourn in Ephesus, a leading city in the Roman province of Asia. During this journey also (although we do
not read of this in Acts) he wrote and sent his letters to the
Corinthians, to the Romans, and probably also to the Gala-
20 tians.
At the beginning of this account, Luke digresses momen-
tarily from Paul's travels to introduce Apollos and to show
how he was instructed in the things of Christ by Paul's
friends Aquila and Priscilla. This is one of several instances
in the book which impresses us with the fact that the work of
God goes on in many places through many people. The Lord
Jesus in continuing the things which He had begun to do
during His earthly ministry was not confined to one locality.
Through the Holy Spirit He was empowering a host of
30 believers for witnessing to the uttermost part of the earth.

The narrative in this part of the book, however, as we have seen, centers upon Paul and his ministry. We read particularly at this juncture of his stay in Ephesus and of what God accomplished through him there. He brought the message of the indwelling Holy Spirit to certain disciples who knew only John's baptism. These were evidently Jews or Jewish proselytes who were confidently looking for Christ, and now that they heard the full message of the gospel, joyously accepted Him.

As his usual practice was, Paul first spoke in the syna- 10 gogue. This he did week after week for three months, until the opposition grew so strong that he had to withdraw. For two years he continued his teaching, using the school of Tyrannus. The word was spread throughout the region. "All they which dwelt in Asia heard the word of the Lord Jesus, both Jews and Greeks" (Acts 19:10). We must remember that *Asia* in the New Testament is not the whole vast continent, but only one province in what we now call Asia Minor.

Here is a demonstration of the power that the Lord Jesus 20 had promised. As credentials of his ministry Paul was enabled by the Lord to perform miracles. This was God's attestation of the message. Great excitement prevailed, many people were saved, and many renounced the Satanic devices of paganism. Paul began to make his plans to continue his travels, purposing to revisit Macedonia and Achaia, then to return to Jerusalem as he had done on his previous tour, and after that, he said, "I must also see Rome" (Acts 19:21). Paul was to see Rome, but not precisely in the way or under the circumstances he anticipated at the time. 30

THE RIOT OF THE SILVERSMITHS

While Paul continued in Ephesus, having sent some of his party ahead into Macedonia (Acts 19:22), he was caught up in a maelstrom of opposition to the gospel. Demetrius, a Gentile, was able to inflame his fellow silversmiths as he did because the gospel had affected all of them where they felt it, as we would say today, in their pocketbooks.

The temple of Artemis (Diana) at Ephesus was one of the reputed seven wonders of the world. The making of little silver shrines of the goddess was one of the city's leading industries. The turning of so many people "to God from idols" (compare I Thessalonians 1:9) threatened the livelihood of the artisans. This was the occasion of the riot described in the passage.

Paul was not permitted by his friends to confront the mob. It is interesting to see that the gospel had had its impact upon some of the rulers of the province:

"And certain of the chief of Asia, which were his friends, sent unto him, desiring him that he would not adventure himself into the theatre" (Acts 19:31).

There is a fine distinction sometimes between bravery and folly. Paul did not lack courage, but to have gone before that howling, unreasoning mob would have been only to invite personal disaster. The people were not open to discussion of any kind; they only kept up their incessant chant, "Great is Diana of the Ephesians" (Acts 19:28, 34). Finally an official succeeded in quieting them long enough to dismiss the illegal assembly, warning them that the city was likely to be called in question by the imperial government, and pointing out that if they had any just grievances they should make use of the duly constituted law courts.

BACK TO FAMILIAR PLACES

Paul's revisiting of the churches established on his previous missionary journey is passed over very briefly. It would be interesting if we could know all the meetings and the conversations that were involved in that time dismissed so quickly in Acts 20:2. What reunions there must have been in the churches of Macedonia, those churches which Paul commends so highly in his Second Epistle to the Corinthians (II Corinthians 8:1-6).

In Greece (Achaia) he remained three months (Acts 20:3), possibly having his headquarters during most of that time in Corinth, the capital city of the province. As always, his bitter enemies, who considered him naturally a traitor and a renegade, sought to bring harm to him (Acts 20:3). Instead of sailing, therefore, as he had planned, he returned overland through Macedonia, thus having opportunity to see many of the Christians there once more. The men mentioned as accompanying him (Acts 20:4) were going because of the offering that had been collected among the Gentile believers as a help to the Jewish believers in Jerusalem. Paul made this an important objective in this period of his ministry, as his epistles reveal.

Luke rejoined Paul at Philippi (Acts 20:5, 6), having remained there apparently for several years from the time of the original visit on the second missionary journey. **10**

The account of the service in Troas shows us something of conditions in the early church. Eutychus, of course, was like ordinary human beings everywhere and in all ages. He cannot be blamed for his sleepiness. But the very fact that Paul was able to preach so long is revelatory of the deep hunger among the believers generally for the Word of God, and of their great affection for the messenger whom God had used so greatly in their lives. **20**

ADDRESS TO THE EPHESIAN ELDERS

The record shows us the indefatigable ministry of Paul. When we remember that he apparently suffered from some kind of chronic illness (see II Corinthians 12:7-10), we realize more fully the sustaining grace of God for him. Determining to be in Jerusalem for the feast of Pentecost he bypassed Ephesus, but sent for the elders of that church to meet him briefly at Miletus. There on the beach he gave one of the most moving messages of his whole career.

Paul has been severely criticized by many Bible students **30** for going to Jerusalem on this trip. He has been accused of stubbornness, self-will and disobedience to God. While we must acknowledge that no man is sinless (except the Man Christ Jesus, who is also Lord of glory), and while we dare not say that Paul was always right in everything he did, we nevertheless ought to judge this matter in the light of the whole context. What Paul says in this address (which even many of those who criticize him accept as inspired Scripture on a par with his writings) does not sound like the deluded stubbornness of a rebellious man out of fellowship with God. He knew by revelation that "bonds and afflictions" were to come (Acts 20:23). In spite of this he had the conviction that this was a part of the course God had given him:

"But none of these things move me, neither count I my life dear unto myself, so that I might finish my course with
10 joy, and the ministry, which I have received of the Lord Jesus, to testify the gospel of the grace of God" (Acts 20:24).

Paul's summary of his ministry in Ephesus gives us a résumé of all his work and a pattern for Christian work generally. Here was no disinterested teacher, presenting the truth and indifferently inviting his hearers to take it or leave it. No, Paul was an advocate for Christ and for His truth with his whole being. His heart was in his message and went out toward his hearers. There was nothing casual
20 about his preaching:

"Wherefore I take you to record this day, that I am pure from the blood of all men. For I have not shunned to declare unto you all the counsel of God. . . . Therefore watch, and remember, that by the space of three years I ceased not to warn every one night and day with tears" (Acts 20:26, 27, 31).

ON TOWARD JERUSALEM

As Paul and his companions continued on their long journey, warnings multiplied of what lay ahead for Paul. At Tyre
30 some of the disciples "said to Paul through the Spirit, that he should not go up to Jerusalem" (Acts 21:4). How is this statement to be interpreted? One interpretation could well be that this was a direct command of God to Paul not to go to Jerusalem. C. I. Scofield (Scofield Reference Edition of the Bible, page 1178) and many other highly respected Bible teachers so interpret it. But this does not seem to take the whole context into account. During the period of

the apostles, before the New Testament was completed, God gave some direct revelations to some of His people ("prophets"). Since Paul was a recipient of such revelations, it seems unlikely that God would tell others, but would not tell Paul, what He wanted him to do. There is no indication that God revealed to Paul any direct command not to go to Jerusalem.

What God did reveal to others, as well as to Paul, was that if Paul went to Jerusalem he would be arrested and imprisoned. The other prophets who received this warning *10* naturally, because of their love for Paul, made a plea for him not to go. Not only those in Tyre, but also Paul's friends at Caesarea, after Agabus had given his warning, entreated him not to go (Acts 21:11, 12). Paul's reply on that occasion was consistent with his actions throughout the period:

"Then Paul answered, What mean ye to weep and to break mine heart? for I am ready not to be bound only, but also to die at Jerusalem for the name of the Lord Jesus" (Acts 21:13). *20*

While we acknowledge the right of anyone to criticize Paul, we would request those critics to accept the situation as Paul's friends did:

"And when he would not be persuaded, we ceased, saying, The will of the Lord be done" (Acts 21:14).

Those who always have an answer for everything, who believe that they can always infallibly pronounce on the rightness or wrongness of the actions of other believers, would do well to criticize an apostle only where God's Word itself criticizes, and would profit from the Holy Spirit's *30* admonition against premature judgments on insufficient grounds:

"Therefore judge nothing before the time, until the Lord come, who both will bring to light the hidden things of darkness, and will make manifest the counsels of the hearts: and then shall every man have praise of God" (I Corinthians 4:5; note the context also).

If Paul was wrong in going to Jerusalem, then he is accountable to the Lord Jesus Christ. Each of us must give account of himself to God (see Romans 14:12). Let us, therefore, be sure that we are obeying the Word of God in our lives.

SQ3R   LESSON 9

1. Where did each of Paul's three missionary journeys begin and end?

   first & began & ended in Antioch 3rd ended in Jerusalem

2. How did Aquila and Priscilla help Apollos?

   they explained things of God more completely

3. How effective was Paul's mission to Ephesus?

   Super!

4. On what ground was opposition stirred up against Paul at Ephesus and by whom, Jews or Gentiles?

   Gentile silversmiths

5. What familiar places did Paul visit after leaving Ephesus?

   _____

6. What are the characteristics of a true church leader as explained by Paul to the Ephesian elders?

   _____

7. In what ways was Paul warned of the dangers which awaited him at Jerusalem?

   _____

Arrested in Jerusalem

The Parthenon on the Acropolis at Athens.

Perry Pictures

YOUR STUDY GUIDE

1. Read the assigned Scripture portion.

2. Take the self-check test based on the Scripture portion.

3. Study the lesson using SQ3R:
   a. Survey the lesson.
   b. Read the SQ3R questions at the end of the lesson.
   c. Read the lesson.
   d. Recite the lesson making marginal notations.
   e. Review the lesson by answering the SQ3R questions boxed in at the end of the lesson.

4. Take the exam.

SCRIPTURE PORTION FOR STUDY

Read Acts 21:18—23:35 twice and then take the following self-check test. Look up the answers to questions in the answer key on page 147.

In the right-hand margin check (√) the following statements "True" or "False" based on your reading of the assigned Scripture portion.

	T	F
1. Paul refused to bow to the wish of the Jerusalem brethren and submit to a Jewish rite.		√
2. A riot against Paul was instigated in the temple precincts by Jews from Asia Minor.	√	
3. The captain of the guard thought that Paul was an Egyptian insurrectionist.	√	
4. Paul was permitted to give his testimony to the Jerusalem mob.	√	
5. Paul was scourged by the chief captain.		√
6. Paul apologized for calling the high priest a "whited wall."	√	√
7. In the midst of his trials in Jerusalem, the Lord encouraged Paul with the promise that he would yet testify for Christ at Rome.	√	
8. Paul's nephew discovered a plot to have Paul assassinated.	√	
9. Paul was given an armed escort out of Jerusalem to Caesarea.	√	
10. When Paul arrived at Caesarea he was set free by the governor.		√

Arrested in Jerusalem

ACTS 21:18—23:35

God works in strange ways. No one would have supposed that the way to Rome lay through Jerusalem. Yet in His overruling providence the all-wise heavenly Father was preparing the scene for the climactic part of the charge of the Lord Jesus:

"Ye shall be witnesses unto me . . . unto the uttermost part of the earth" (Acts 1:8).

10 Often we read the Bible too matter-of-factly. We need to gain or regain a sense of wonder at the wonder-working power of God and to allow ourselves to be caught up in these moving events of the spread of the gospel.

Some men would say that this was all wasted effort and wasted time; that if Paul had not gone to Jerusalem he could have gone to Rome much sooner, and not as a prisoner. Let us be careful how we judge; in fact, let us suspend judgment about this particular matter altogether and simply marvel at the delivering and all-pervasive grace of God.

20 PAUL IN JERUSALEM

Paul's last recorded visit to Jerusalem was filled with turmoil.

After arriving in Jerusalem Paul gave a report to James and the elders of the church concerning his ministry among the Gentiles (Acts 21:18, 19). Their response was to give glory to God.

The next event is another of those controversial situations which seem to cluster around Paul. Some Bible teachers are horrified that the apostle of Christian liberty would 30 participate in any of the rituals of Judaism. It is not likely that Paul was denying anything that he had written or spoken on the subject. He evidently was not aware of any inconsistency. This seems to have been, rather, an instance of his following the principle which he had previously laid down:

"For though I be free from all men, yet have I made myself servant unto all, that I might gain the more. And unto the Jews I became as a Jew, that I might gain the Jews; to them that are under the law, as under the law, that I might gain them that are under the law" (I Corinthians 9:19, 20).

PAUL'S ARREST IN THE TEMPLE 10

Probably not too many people in Jerusalem would have known or recognized Paul at this time. Years had elapsed since his previous visit. However, some Jews from Asia, who would have known of his preaching in Ephesus, recognized him and stirred up the multitude against him. They made the untrue accusation that he had brought Gentiles into the temple, because they had seen Trophimus, who was from Ephesus, with him previously in the city (Acts 21:29).

Paul could be thankful for the Roman constabulary, otherwise he would have been killed by the angry mob. The 20 Roman officer in charge, without interrogating him, had him bound with chains. Later he was astonished that Paul could speak Greek, because he had jumped to the conclusion that Paul was a notorious Egyptian criminal insurrectionist. After Paul had identified himself, he was permitted to speak to the crowd.

PAUL'S DEFENSE TO THE CROWD

In his speech from the stairs in the Jerusalem street Paul rehearsed his life and his conversion, repeating that which has already been placed into the record, as we have previous- 30 ly seen. The crowd listened as he told these things. Then he recounted a previous visit to Jerusalem, probably the first one after his conversion, and told of the words of the Lord Jesus to him on that occasion:

"Depart: for I will send thee far hence unto the Gentiles" (Acts 22:21).

That was all the mob would take. When he came to that point, when he mentioned the hated Gentiles as the object of his mission, the Jews quickly interrupted and came near to violence again. Again the Roman officer intervened and determined that he would question Paul. His plan was to use the regular method of questioning by scourging, since it was believed that this was the only way to get at the truth. Paul's question to the centurion, repeated to the chief captain, brought a change in tactics. The word *Roman* was
10 like a magic word in a situation like this. The highly prized Roman citizenship which Paul possessed from birth was of great value in these circumstances. Paul did not hesitate to take advantage of it. Wishing to learn what the charges were against Paul, the official brought him the next day before the Jewish council.

PAUL BEFORE THE SANHEDRIN

One wonders if Paul thought of Stephen on this occasion, Stephen with the shining countenance like that of an angel, Stephen endued with the boldness of the Holy Spirit. He
20 must have. How much had happened since that long-ago day!

It is uncertain why Paul did not recognize the high priest, who would presumably have been wearing the distinctive garb of his office. Some have surmised that Paul had poor eyesight, but of this we cannot be sure.

Knowing the bitter division between the Pharisees and the Sadducees, Paul made an appeal to a doctrine on which he and the Pharisees could agree—the fact of the resurrection of the dead. Again, some have accused Paul of com-
30 promise for identifying himself with the unbelieving Pharisees, but no compromise was involved. On this point the Pharisees were perfectly orthodox, in contrast to the rationalistic Sadducees. Paul was following the instruction of the Lord, who had defeated both the Pharisees and the Sadducees in debate (see, for example, Matthew 22:23-46) and who had told His disciples to be "wise as serpents, and harmless as doves" (Matthew 10:16).

115

Paul knew all along that he had broken no law, but that he could never receive a fair trial from the Jewish religious leaders, and that his only recourse, humanly speaking, was to make use of his Roman citizenship. Again Rome came to the rescue (Acts 23:10), pulling the apostle away from those who would have torn him to pieces. There is a divine irony in the thought of Caesar's legions unwittingly performing the service of God.

THE PLOT AGAINST PAUL

There is no reproach, only encouragement, in the words the *10* Lord Jesus spoke to Paul that night in Jerusalem:

"Be of good cheer, Paul: for as thou hast testified of me in Jerusalem, so must thou bear witness also at Rome" (Acts 23:11).

For years Paul had been looking toward that goal. When he wrote his Epistle to the Romans while on his third missionary journey, he told of this long-held desire:

"Making request, if by any means now at length I might have a prosperous journey by the will of God to come unto you. . . . Now I would not have you ignorant, brethren, that *20* oftentimes I purposed to come unto you, (but was let [hindered] hitherto,) that I might have some fruit among you also, even as among other Gentiles" (Romans 1:10, 13).

"But now having no more place in these parts, and having a great desire these many years to come unto you; whensoever I take my journey into Spain, I will come to you" (Romans 15:23, 24).

It was not to work out exactly as Paul himself had planned. Nevertheless his arrival in Rome was certain; the Lord Jesus Himself had now made that clear. With this *30* assurance Paul could face hostile councils, murderous plots, avaricious governors and lackadaisical kings.

More than forty fanatical men now banded themselves together in a plot to kill Paul, binding themselves by an oath to abstain from food and drink until their purpose was accomplished. The plot involved the conscious and willing connivance of the religious leaders. Paul's nephew, in some

116

way of which we are not informed, learned of the plot, made it known to Paul, and then at his request revealed it to the Roman officer, Claudius Lysias.

Again we enjoy the spectacle of the massed power of the worldly empire protecting the lone servant of Christ. Two hundred soldiers, seventy horsemen and two hundred spearmen were deployed to escort the prisoner to Caesarea, where he would be brought before the Roman governor.

Claudius Lysias seems to have been a reasonable man. He rightly concluded, in his letter to the governor, that Paul had done nothing criminal. Paul was really in a kind of protective custody. Felix the governor, after a preliminary questioning, remanded the prisoner for trial at such time as his accusers would appear.

Some might believe that everything was lost. Paul was a prisoner, his ministry seemingly halted, his very life in jeopardy. But Paul had that promise from the Lord, a promise that sustained him during the ensuing two long years at Caesarea: "So must thou bear witness also at Rome" (Acts 23:11). Paul knew the truth of what he had written: "We walk by faith, not by sight" (II Corinthians 5:7). How often we seem to prefer to walk by sight, and how discouraged we become in the face of obstacles!

If one may be permitted some levity about a serious subject, one could wonder about the forty-odd conspirators. Did they really starve to death?

SQ3R   LESSON 10

1. To what extent did Paul compromise conviction in submitting to Jewish ritual at Jerusalem?

_____

2. Why was Paul arrested?

_____

3. How did Paul defend the gospel before the mob and later before the Sanhedrin?

_____

4. Who discovered the plot against Paul and how was it foiled?

_____

The Two Years in Caesarea

The Colosseum in Rome.

Perry Pictures

YOUR STUDY GUIDE

1. Read the assigned Scripture portion.

2. Take the self-check test based on the Scripture portion.

3. Study the lesson using SQ3R:
   a. Survey the lesson.
   b. Read the SQ3R questions at the end of the lesson.
   c. Read the lesson.
   d. Recite the lesson making marginal notations.
   e. Review the lesson by answering the SQ3R questions boxed in at the end of the lesson.

4. Take the exam.

SCRIPTURE PORTION FOR STUDY

Read Acts 24, 25 and 26 twice and then take the following self-check test. Look up the answers to questions in the answer key on page 147.

SELF-CHECK TEST 11

In the right-hand margin check (√) the following statements "True" or "False" based on your reading of the assigned Scripture portion.

		T	F
1.	The orator employed by the Jews to plead their case against Paul was Tertullus.	T	
2.	Paul addressed Felix in a most courteous manner.	T	
3.	Felix hoped that Paul would bribe him to set him at liberty.	T	
4.	When Festus wanted Paul to go to Jerusalem to be tried, Paul agreed.		F
5.	Festus was somewhat out of his depth when it came to deciding what to do about Paul.	T	
6.	Paul told King Agrippa that he was happy to have the opportunity of telling him his story.	T	
7.	Paul asked Agrippa why it should be thought a thing incredible that God should raise the dead.	T	F
8.	As Festus listened to Paul's speech to Agrippa, he was favorably impressed by Paul's defense.		F
9.	Paul urged Agrippa to become a Christian.	T	F
10.	Agrippa told Festus that Paul was worthy of death.		F

The Two Years in Caesarea

ACTS 24—26

Two years seems a long time to be at the whim of a Roman governor. But God has His purposes which are far above the understanding of the men of this world. During the whole period Paul was permitted to have the company of his friends and acquaintances. Many scholars believe it was during this time that Luke, in frequent consultation with
10 Paul, produced his first book, the "former treatise" (see Acts 1:1), which we know as the Gospel According to Luke. At any rate we can be sure that in the economy of eternity the two years were not wasted.

PAUL BEFORE FELIX

Felix occupied the same position that Pontius Pilate had held when the Lord Jesus was crucified about thirty years before the events in this section. The official Roman capital of the province of Judea was at Caesarea.

The chief priests lost little time in prosecuting their case
20 against Paul. Tertullus, who spoke before the governor for them, was apparently a well-known lawyer. He began by flattering Felix and then proceeded to try to link Paul with sedition and sacrilege. He indicated that the Jewish religious leaders could have settled the case themselves if Claudius Lysias had not taken Paul out of their hands.

Paul, being permitted to speak in his own defense, gave a straightforward, unvarnished account of the events of the last twelve days. He confessed that he worshiped the God of his fathers; the difference between him and these other

Jews was that he actually believed all that was written in the law and the prophets. He told of the purpose of his coming to Jerusalem, a benevolent and unselfish one (Acts 24:17).

Felix was married to Drusilla, a Jewess (Acts 24:24), who was in fact the sister of King Agrippa and Bernice. Consequently he knew something of the Jewish religion. He realized that Paul was no criminal; yet he did not set him free. We see a strange mixture in his character. He treated Paul well, permitting him as much liberty as possible *10* for a prisoner (Acts 24:23). When Paul spoke to him of Christ, he trembled with fear, yet he would not accept the Saviour. His reaction was that of so many people, putting off acceptance of Christ until another time, which unhappily never comes:

"Go thy way for this time; when I have a convenient season, I will call for thee" (Acts 24:25).
There never is any convenient season for many like Felix. Soon it is too late.

Nevertheless Felix kept summoning Paul before him, not *20* now to be instructed in the things of Christ, but as a means of extortion. Somehow the governor thought that Paul could or would pay for his release, and he was not above accepting such a bribe. Two whole years passed. Felix' term ended, and as he was replaced by Porcius Festus, he left Paul a prisoner, "willing to show the Jews a pleasure" (Acts 24:27).

PAUL BEFORE FESTUS

Almost as soon as Festus had been inducted into office he made a trip to Jerusalem to confer with the Jewish leaders. *30* They renewed their old plea that Paul might be turned over to them for a religious trial, although their plan, as before, was that he should be disposed of before the trial could take place. Whatever Festus' personal character may have been, he upheld the dignity and authority of Roman law by requiring Paul's enemies to appear before him in Caesarea and to accuse Paul in open court.

As before, the Jews "laid many and grievous complaints against Paul, which they could not prove" (Acts 25:7). This is one of the most dramatic scenes in this whole dramatic book. To the formal question whether Paul would be willing to answer before the Jewish tribunal in Jerusalem, Paul gave a formal and decisive reply:

"Then said Paul, I stand at Caesar's judgment seat, where I ought to be judged: to the Jews have I done no wrong, as thou very well knowest. For if I be an offender, or have
10 committed any thing worthy of death, I refuse not to die: but if there be none of these things whereof these accuse me, no man may deliver me unto them. I appeal unto Caesar" (Acts 25:10, 11).

This was the cherished, time-honored right of every Roman citizen, to appeal his case to the highest court in the empire, to the emperor himself. Festus and his council readily granted the appeal, setting the legal machinery in motion which would guarantee that Paul would go to Rome, there to present his case.

20 PAUL BEFORE AGRIPPA

The King Agrippa mentioned here was Herod Agrippa II, the son of Herod Agrippa I, whose death is described in chapter 12. During Agrippa's visit Festus told him about this troublesome prisoner, who really had not done anything illegal, but who could not be released because of the intense feeling of the Jews against him.

Festus gives the impression throughout the account of being a man beyond his depth in affairs that swirl about him. He made a firm and somewhat disdainful statement of
30 Roman justice (Acts 25:16) to the Jewish leaders, who were not particularly interested in the fine points of law; yet apparently he would have been willing to turn Paul over to them (Acts 25:20)—as a convenient way of getting rid of the problem—if Paul had not insisted on his rights as a Roman citizen. Later, as Paul spoke before Agrippa and the assembled company, Festus could think of him only

as a madman (Acts 26:24). Festus was only one of a long line of little men in large places in this sin-cursed world.

With all his shortcomings Festus had sense enough to realize that it would be ridiculous to send a prisoner to Caesar without having some charge against him. There were no charges against Paul, except some made-up ones, the falsity of which was perfectly obvious both to Felix and to Festus. Hence the governor did not know what to write to the imperial court. The hearing before Agrippa, therefore, took on something of the nature of a formal court   10
hearing even though Agrippa did not have legal jurisdiction in the case.

If ever the grace of God was seen in a man it was seen in Paul. And this was one of his greatest hours. The Lord Jesus had told him that he was to bear the message before kings, and here he was, comporting himself with politeness and dignity, with no hint of flattery or obsequiousness. Making what seems to have been a characteristic gesture (Acts 26:1), he began his story.

The theme of this address, as well as of Paul's whole   20
Christian life, may be summed up in his words to Agrippa: "Whereupon, O king Agrippa, I was not disobedient unto the heavenly vision" (Acts 26:19). As we have noted earlier in our study, there is a repetition here of Paul's conversion experience, recorded for the first time in chapter 9 and repeated in the address to the Jerusalem mob in chapter 22. Note that Paul makes everything hinge on the resurrection of Christ. This was the proof and the seal of our Lord's redemptive work on the cross. Paul showed that the Old Testament Scriptures clearly foretold the gospel: 30

"I continue unto this day, witnessing both to small and great, saying none other things than those which the prophets and Moses did say should come: that Christ should suffer, and that he should be the first that should rise from the dead, and should show light unto the people, and to the Gentiles" (Acts 26:22, 23).

To Festus' loud exclamation that his great learning had turned him to madness, Paul answered with dignified restraint and appealed to Agrippa's background and knowledge of events. He knew that Agrippa, who was a Jew, prided himself on his knowledge of Jewish affairs, and he pointed out that the events connected with the Lord Jesus Christ had not taken place privately but in the full glare of publicity.

This was not an academic matter with Paul, nor was it merely a personal defense. He turned it into an evangelistic appeal: "King Agrippa, believest thou the prophets? I know that thou believest" (Acts 26:27).

The king's reply was enigmatical. Was he saying that he really was almost persuaded of the truth of the gospel, or was he cynically implying that it would take more than this to make *him* a Christian? Was he speaking wistfully or scornfully? Were his words serious or frivolous? We cannot be sure. Paul, however, chose to interpret his statement seriously, for he replied with great earnestness:

"I would to God, that not only thou, but also all that hear me this day, were both almost, and altogether such as I am, except these bonds" (Acts 26:29).

This ended the audience, and we see as so often in human experience the tragedy of the uncommitted, even of the almost committed. Combining the responses of Felix and Agrippa, Philip P. Bliss wrote the well-known gospel song:

> "Almost persuaded" now to believe;
> "Almost persuaded" Christ to receive;
> Seems now some soul to say,
> "Go, Spirit, go Thy way,
> Some more convenient day
>   On Thee I'll call."
>
> "Almost persuaded," come, come today;
> "Almost persuaded," turn not away;
> Jesus invites you here,
> Angels are lingering near,
> Prayers rise from hearts so dear,
>   O wanderer, come.
>
> "Almost persuaded," harvest is past!
> "Almost persuaded," doom comes at last!
> "Almost" cannot avail;

129

"Almost" is but to fail!
Sad, sad that bitter wail,
"Almost"—but lost.

Both Felix and Agrippa, as well as matter-of-fact Festus, stand in the eternal Word of God as warning examples to other men. They had the glorious opportunity to accept Christ, but they would not.

The Bible is filled with strange and unusual twists of events which portray a divine irony. All who had heard Paul were agreed that he had done "nothing worthy of 10 death or of bonds" (Acts 26:31). Agrippa's conclusion might cause one to be torn between laughter and tears: "This man might have been set at liberty, if he had not appealed unto Caesar" (Acts 26:32)!

What should be the reaction of a Christian? Should one bemoan the fact that Paul had been so foolish as to appeal to Caesar? No, of course not, for that had not been a foolish action at all. It was the right thing, the only thing he could have done at the time he did it.

Should we expect that Paul should be filled with remorse 20 and bitterness? No, for Paul had the promise of the Lord Jesus that he should bear testimony in Rome, and now he could see how the Lord was going to get him there. Caesar was going to pay the bill. This was not a defeat for Paul or the gospel. "God moves in a mysterious way His wonders to perform." If we are only yielded to Him, we shall become aware of His hand in all the happenings of life. Here was no blind fate against which to rail, but a heavenly Father's providence for which to give thanks.

SQ3R   LESSON 11

1. How long was Paul detained at Caesarea?

    _____

2. Why did Felix keep summoning Paul before him?

    _____

3. What was the attitude of Festus to Paul?

    _____

4. What is the significance of Paul's appeal to Caesar?

    _____

5. Why was Festus eager to have King Agrippa give Paul
    a hearing?

    _____

6. How did King Agrippa respond to Paul's testimony
    and appeal?

    _____

The Journey to Rome

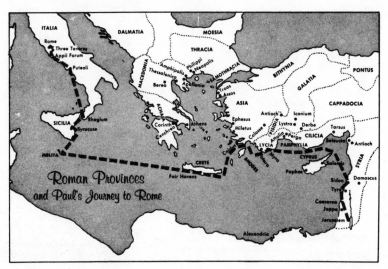

Roman Provinces and Paul's Journey to Rome

YOUR STUDY GUIDE

1. Read the assigned Scripture portion.

2. Take the self-check test based on the Scripture portion.

3. Study the lesson using SQ3R:
   a. Survey the lesson.
   b. Read the SQ3R questions at the end of the lesson.
   c. Read the lesson.
   d. Recite the lesson making marginal notations.
   e. Review the lesson by answering the SQ3R questions boxed in at the end of the lesson.

4. Take the exam.

SCRIPTURE PORTION FOR STUDY

Read Acts 27 and 28 twice and then take the following self-check test. Look up the answers to questions in the answer key on page 147.

SELF-CHECK TEST 12

In the right-hand margin check (√) the following statements "True" or "False" based on your reading of the assigned Scripture portion.

	T	F
1. The centurion in charge of Paul's convoy to Rome was Augustus.		✓
2. Luke accompanied Paul to Rome.	✓	
3. At Fair Havens the centurion believed Paul rather than the ship's captain.	✓	
4. Paul was shipwrecked on the island of Crete.		✓
5. The only prisoner who escaped the shipwreck was Paul.		✓
6. Publius was the chief of the island on which Paul and his companions were shipwrecked.	✓	
7. Paul suffered severely from a snake bite when gathering sticks for a fire on the island.		✓
8. Believers from Rome met Paul at a place called Appii Forum.	✓	✗
9. Although a prisoner, Paul continued to witness for Christ at Rome.	✓	
10. Paul was incarcerated in the common prison at Rome.		✓

134

The Journey to Rome

ACTS 27, 28

In this study of the book of Acts we have, of course, only skimmed the surface. Our purpose has been to become acquainted with the factual content of the book, especially as it centers around the two apostles Peter and Paul in their respective spheres of ministry.

We have traced the spread of the gospel according to the pattern given by the Lord Jesus Christ just before His
10 ascension to heaven: in Jerusalem and Judea, in Samaria, and to the uttermost part of the earth (Acts 1:8).

We have already seen that the book does not purport to tell of the ministries of all the apostles, or even to give the complete stories of those relatively few Christians whose careers it follows. We are not told of every distant place and clime to which the gospel was taken.

Nevertheless we have been moving toward a climax. From chapter 13 on, the center has shifted from Jerusalem and the evangelization of the Jews primarily, to Antioch
20 and the world-wide missionary effort among the Gentiles. The climax is exemplified by Rome, the imperial city. The Romans proudly boasted, "All roads lead to Rome." Conversely, all roads led *from* there. Once the gospel was firmly based in the capital it could spread rapidly from there in all directions.

In this last lesson of our study we shall note that the close of the book is in Rome, with the message still going out both to Jews and Gentiles.

BEGINNING OF THE VOYAGE

30 The last "we" section in the book begins with chapter 27. Paul's going to Rome had been set, and Luke accompanied

135

him. It will be of help to you to trace the journey to Rome on the map. Paul, of course, was technically a prisoner. Julius, the centurion who was in charge of a group of prisoners on this trip, treated Paul most courteously, giving him liberties that a prisoner would not ordinarily have enjoyed.

This portion of the book gives a further glimpse of the extent of travel in the first century. We have observed this previously both by land and by sea; here we see ships plying back and forth in the Mediterranean Sea carrying both 10 freight and passengers. Luke gives a circumstantial account of the different ships that were used and the different places visited.

The early part of the voyage was in the autumn, probably in the year 62. Looking back, this means that Paul's arrest and his first appearance before Felix had probably been in the year 60. We know the time of year for the beginning of the voyage from the mention of the "fast" (Acts 27:9), which was the great Day of Atonement, and also from Paul's entreaty that the ship should winter at Fair Havens. 20

THE STORM AND SHIPWRECK

The storm which came upon them was an exceedingly fierce one. Even the experienced sailors despaired. All hope was gone (Acts 27:20). Paul then gave encouragement, not the sort of false encouragement that the world knows as "whistling in the dark," but encouragement that was genuine because it came from God Himself. An angel from God had told Paul:

"Fear not, Paul; thou must be brought before Caesar: and, lo, God hath given thee all them that sail with thee" 30 (Acts 27:24).

In response to this, Paul's word to those with him on the ship was:

"Wherefore, sirs, be of good cheer: for I believe God, that it shall be even as it was told me" (Acts 27:25).
Believing God is the essential, no matter what the circumstances may be.

As the ship lay in shallow water with four anchors holding it, the sailors tried to save themselves by letting down the ship's boat and seeking to desert the ship and the passengers. At Paul's word to the centurion, the soldiers prevented this desertion. After the ship was grounded and was breaking up, the soldiers wanted to kill the prisoners to prevent their escaping. Julius, the centurion, who already had shown himself to be Paul's friend, kept them from their purpose, thus saving Paul's life and the lives of all the rest.
10 As God had promised, "they escaped all safe to land" (Acts 27:44).

This was only one of the many dangers through which Paul passed in his years of service for the Lord Jesus Christ. The catalogue of his experiences which he gave to the Corinthians included, among other things, three shipwrecks and "a night and a day . . . in the deep" (II Corinthians 11:25). That was written some years before this event.

EXPERIENCES ON MELITA

The island on which Paul and his companions were ship-
20 wrecked was the present-day Malta. The fact that the inhabitants are called barbarians simply means that they were not Greek-speaking; it does not imply that they were savages. The incident of the viper shows their superstition, as they quickly changed their opinion about Paul (Acts 28:3-6). It also is confirmation of the words of the Lord Jesus concerning the signs that would be evident in connection with the preaching of the gospel (Mark 16:18).

Another such sign was the miracle of the healing of the father of Publius, the chief man of the island. No doubt
30 this and the ensuing miracles provided a sympathetic hearing for the gospel during the three months the travelers were on Melita.

With the coming of spring the centurion and his charges sailed on another ship, the *Castor and Pollux,* which had wintered on the island (Acts 28:11).

137

ROME AT LAST

After landing in Italy, Paul was met by Christians who were a source of great encouragement to him. At Rome he was delivered by Julius to the captain of the guard, but his status was such that he was permitted to live in a private dwelling, even though he was under constant guard. This made possible his active preaching of the gospel. His first move was to call together the leading men of the Jewish community, in order to explain his situation and to present Christ to them.   *10*

One of the unexplained circumstances is that these Jewish leaders in Rome had had no word from Judea concerning Paul. We can hardly imagine that those religious leaders who had sought his life in Judea would have failed to send a message to Rome concerning him as soon as they knew he would be sent there. It is possible that a messenger, coming at about the same time on another ship, might have been lost at sea, but this is only speculation. Whatever the cause of their not having heard about Paul, these Jewish leaders in Rome were at first willing to hear what he had   *20* to say.

It must have been a great occasion when Paul expounded the Scriptures all day to those who came:

"And when they had appointed him a day, there came many to him into his lodging; to whom he expounded and testified the kingdom of God, persuading them concerning Jesus, both out of the law of Moses, and out of the prophets, from morning till evening" (Acts 28:23).

The reception was mixed, some believing and some not believing. The tragedy of Israel's unbelief as a nation is   *30* set forth in all its stark reality here at the close of the book of Acts.

Paul had always given the Jews an opportunity to accept Christ. To the Romans he had written that the gospel "is the power of God unto salvation to every one that believeth; to the Jew first, and also to the Greek" (Romans 1:16). The statement of God's judgment upon the nation of Israel for unbelief is quoted from the book of Isaiah (Acts 28:25-27; compare Isaiah 6:9, 10).

Since most of those to whom the gospel was first preached refused it, it was to be given to those who would listen:

"Be it known therefore unto you, that the salvation of God is sent unto the Gentiles, and that they will hear it" (Acts 28:28).

The message of Christ was going out to the ends of the earth, as the Old Testament prophet Isaiah had prophesied
10 and as the Lord Jesus Christ had commanded.

NOT THE END OF THE STORY

The book of Acts closes with Paul still a prisoner in Rome after two years, living "in his own hired house," receiving "all that came in unto him, preaching the kingdom of God, and teaching those things which concern the Lord Jesus Christ, with all confidence, no man forbidding him" (Acts 28:30, 31).

During the two years mentioned in the passage many things occurred, even though Paul was awaiting trial. (Ap-
20 parently it is not only in modern times that courts are often slow.) Among other things, he wrote his epistles to the Ephesians, to the Colossians, to Philemon and to the Philippians. In writing to the Philippians, possibly toward the close of this two-year period, Paul told of the progress of the gospel in Rome:

"But I would ye should understand, brethren, that the things which happened unto me have fallen out rather unto the furtherance of the gospel; so that my bonds in Christ are manifest in all the palace, and in all other places"
30 (Philippians 1:12, 13).

At that time he looked forward confidently to his release (Philippians 1:25, 26). We have reason to believe that Paul was acquitted at his trial, that he was released, and that he continued his journeys for Christ. His First Epistle to Timothy and his Epistle to Titus belong to that period. Still later, we believe, he was arrested again, and this time was

139

imprisoned in a dungeon in Rome, from which he wrote his last letter, the Second Epistle to Timothy. None of the things mentioned in this paragraph, however, is included in the book of Acts.

Why does Acts end so abruptly? In fact, the book hardly seems to have a formal close at all. The Holy Spirit directed Luke to break off the story at this point that it might be recorded and go out while the events were still going on. This is not really the end of anything. God wants to impress upon us that there is no real close to the *acts* which the 10 Lord Jesus continues to do as long as the church is in this world. The messengers are taken away one by one, but the message goes on. Throughout the centuries the risen Christ has been continuing His work through His disciples by the power of the Holy Spirit.

SQ3R LESSON 12

1. How does the book of Acts move toward a climax?

   By the gospel preached in Rome

2. Who accompanied Paul to Rome?

   Luke.

3. How did the centurion Julius treat Paul?

   Considerately

4. How do we know what time of year it was when they set sail for Rome?

   Because "the time of the fast" is mentioned

5. How many times was Paul shipwrecked?

   _3_

6. Who was Publius?

   _____

7. What reason is suggested to account for the Jewish leaders in Rome not having heard of Paul?

   _____

8. How long had Paul been detained at Rome when the book of Acts closes?

   2 yrs.

141

answer key
to self-check tests

Be sure to look up any questions you answered incorrectly.

Q gives the number of the test *question*.

A gives the correct *answer*.

R *refers* you back to the Scripture reference where the correct answer is to be found.

Mark your wrong answers with an "x".

Q	TEST 1 A R	TEST 2 A R	TEST 3 A R	TEST 4 A R	TEST 5 A R	TEST 6 A R
1	F 1:3	T 3:2	F 6:3	T 9:1	F 10:1	T 11:26; 13:2
2	T 1:8	F 3:8	T 6:3,8	T 9:4	T 10:16,19	F 13:10
3	F 1:12	F 3:12	T 6:10,11, 13	T 9:6	T 10:45,46	F 13:14; 14:1
4	F 1:26	F 4:13	T 7:1-55	F 9:13	F 11:1-3	T 13:42-48
5	T 2:2,3	F 4:16	T 7:55	T 9:17	F 11:19,20	T 13:51
6	F 2:6-8	T 4:36,37	F 7:60	T 9:23	T 11:26	T 14:1,2,6 19
7	T 2:16	F 5:2	F 8:1,3	F 9:26	T 11:22,23	T 14:8
8	T 2:41	T 5:11	T 8:13	T 9:31	T 11:25,26	T 14:11
9	T 2:41,42	T 5:19	T 8:32,33	T 9:36-41	T 12:11	F 14:21-26
10	F 2:47	T 5:34-39	F 8:36-38	T 9:43	F 12:12-16	F 14:28

Q	TEST 7 A R	TEST 8 A R	TEST 9 A R	TEST 10 A R	TEST 11 A R	TEST 12 A R
1	F 15:1	T 15:37-39	T 18:26	F 21:23-26	T 24:1	F 27:1
2	T 15:6	T 16:1-3	F 19:14-16	T 21:27	T 24:10	T 27:1
3	T 15:5,6	T 16:8,9	T 19:19	T 21:38	T 24:26	F 27:11
4	F 15:10,11	T 16:14	F 20:1	T 22:1-21	F 25:9-11	F 27:13
5	T 15:12	F 16:27-29	F 20:3	F 22:24-29	T 25:20,26	F 27:42-44
6	T 15:19	T 17:5,13	T 20:9-12	T 23:3-6	T 26:1,2	T 28:7
7	T 15:23-27	F 17:32-34	T 20:26	T 23:11	T 26:8	F 28:5
8	F 15:30,31	F 18:2,3	F 20:38	T 23:16	F 26:24	T 28:15
9	T 15:27,32	T 18:12	T 21:11	T 23:23,24	T 26:27-29	T 28:17-28
10	T 15:40	F 18:19,20	T 21:17	F 23:35	F 26:31	F 28:30

How well did you do?

0-1 wrong answer—excellent work

2-3 wrong answers—review errors carefully

4 or more wrong answers—restudy the lesson before going on to the next one

BIBLIOGRAPHY

The following books are recommended to help you in further study of the book of Acts. They may be obtained from your local Christian bookstore or from Moody Bookstore, 820 N. LaSalle Street, Chicago, Illinois 60610.

IRONSIDE, H. A., *Lectures on Acts*. New York: Loizeaux Brothers. Popular treatment. Very readable.

MORGAN, G. CAMPBELL, *The Acts of the Apostles*. New York: Fleming H. Revell. Paragraph studies by "the prince of expositors." Excellent unfolding of Acts.

RYRIE, CHARLES C., *The Acts of the Apostles*. Chicago: Moody Press. Outline studies on a basic level.

BRUCE, F. F., *The Book of Acts*, in *The New London Commentary on the New Testament*. Grand Rapids, Michigan: Wm. B. Eerdmans; reprint, 1956. Thorough and readable by an outstanding evangelical scholar.

RAMSAY, Wm. M., *St. Paul, the Traveller and the Roman Citizen*. Grand Rapids, Michigan: Baker Book House; reprint, 1960. Excellent background reading written by a renowned archaeologist.

ERDMAN, CHARLES R., *The Acts: An Exposition*. Philadelphia: The Westminster Press; 1920. A brief review of the early church.

GAEBELEIN, A. C., *The Acts of the Apostles: An Exposition*. Neptune, New Jersey: Loizeaux Brothers; 1912. An interpretive study.

LENSKI, R. C. H., *The Interpretation of the Acts of the Apostles*. Minneapolis, Minnesota: Augsburg Publishing House; 1934. A thorough examination of Acts with a new translation.

THOMAS, W. H. GRIFFITH, *Outline Studies in Acts*. Grand Rapids, Michigan: Wm. B. Eerdmans; 1956. A scholarly work by a well known author.

WHO, ME...

lead a Bible study class? YES...why not?

After completing this course, why not expand your ministry by sharing the truths you have learned with your friends?

It's easy to organize a class in your home or church. Moody Correspondence School will provide valuable taped lectures, discussion guides and personal attention to help you and your class study God's Word.

CLASS LEADERS RECEIVE HELP

√ *Taped Lectures* bring a Moody professor into your class. Selected teachers have recorded 15-minute messages to go along with each lesson of some of our Bible study courses. As you and your friends gather for Bible study, you listen to the Bible scholar teach the lesson and then all join in the discussion period.

√ *Teacher's Supplements* for most popular-level courses help make each class session a true learning situation.

√ *A Teacher's Guide* gives suggestions on how to prepare interesting and worthwhile lessons.

√ *A Trained Instructor* gives counsel and guidance. A letter or a phone call brings instant help. Your teaching is undergirded by Moody's decades of teaching experience.

STUDENTS RECEIVE HELP

√ Top quality textbooks

√ Thought-provoking exams and tests to measure progress

√ Added instruction from Moody—help and encouragement from a trained instructor

√ Valuable certificates to award achievement

√ The status of studying with a world-famous school, a pioneer in Christian education

CLASSES RECEIVE A DISCOUNT

5 to 19 students	10 percent
20 to 49 students	15 percent
50 or more students	20 percent

fill out the application on the next page

Application for
CLASS ENROLLMENT

Please enroll the following class.

Course title_____

Group (Sunday school, etc.)_____

Class leader   ☐ Rev.   ☐ Mr.   ☐ Mrs.   ☐ Miss

Name_____

Address_____

City_____State_____Zip_____

Church_____

Please send the following materials:

_____Textbooks @ $_____
      (Deduct class discount.)

_____Teacher's supplements @ $2.00

___Acts—Power for Witnessing

___Apostasy Unmasked
    A Study in Jude

___Beginning with Genesis

___Cults Exposed

___Daniel—The Framework
    of Prophecy

___Exploring Christianity

___First Steps in the
    Christian Faith

___God's Will for Your Life

___Hebrews—From Shadow
    to Substance

___Isaiah—A Study in Events
    to Come

___John—Life Through Believing

___Psalms—Songs of Praises

___Redemption in Exodus

___Revelation—God's Final
    Word to Man

___Successful Soul-Winning

___Survey of the Scriptures—
    Part 1

___Survey of the Scriptures—
    Part 2

___Survey of the Scriptures—
    Part 3

___Teaching—With Results

___The Bible Says . . .

___The Good News

___The Gospel in Galatians

___The Person and Work of
    the Holy Spirit

___Understanding and
    Guiding the Student

_____Teacher's Guide (Gives helpful suggestions on how to conduct
any class. $1.00)

_____Bulletin covers @ $2.00 per 100   _____

_____Display posters @ $ .10 each   _____
      Postage and handling fees   _____

                                                TOTAL COST $_____

☐ Payment enclosed.   ☐ Please bill me.

Signed_____